THE PUBLICATIONS COMMITEE OF THE COUNCIL

Twentysixth annual report of the Council of Missions

Cooperating with the Church of Christ in Japan

THE PUBLICATIONS COMMITEE OF THE COUNCIL

Twentysixth annual report of the Council of Missions
Cooperating with the Church of Christ in Japan

ISBN/EAN: 9783741169274

Manufactured in Europe, USA, Canada, Australia, Japa

Cover: Foto ©Andreas Hilbeck / pixelio.de

Manufactured and distributed by brebook publishing software (www.brebook.com)

THE PUBLICATIONS COMMITEE OF THE COUNCIL

Twentysixth annual report of the Council of Missions

TWENTY-SIXTH
ANNUAL REPORT OF THE COUNCIL
OF MISSIONS

COÖPERATING WITH THE

CHURCH OF CHRIST IN JAPAN

ISSUED BY THE PUBLICATIONS COMMITTEE

OF THE COUNCIL

1903

FUKUIN PRINTING COMPANY, LTD.
YOKOHAMA JAPAN.

OFFICERS OF THE COUNCIL
FOR 1903-1904

ESIDENT . . . . D. B. Schneder
CE PRESIDENT . . George P. Pierson
CRETARY . . H. W. Myers
EASURER .. . . . John C. Ballagh

PUBLICATIONS COMMITTEE

William Imbrie
Albert Oltmans
S. P. Fulton
A. D. Hail
J. P. Moore

SECRETARIES

OF THE

COÖPERATING MISSIONS

William Imbrie	Tokyo
Harvey Brokaw	Hiroshima
M. N. Wyckoff	Tokyo
Henry Stout	Nagasaki
Charles A. Logan	Tokushima
Paul L. Gerhard	Sendai
A. D. Hail	Osaka
Miss Julia E. Hand	Yokohama

CONTENTS

I PROCEEDINGS OF THE COUNCIL
  1 OPENING AND SESSIONS OF THE COUNCIL.   1
  2 REPORTS OF STANDING COMMITTEES

    Publications 2
    Sunday-school literature 2
    Statistics 4
    Report of Treasurer 4

  3 REPORTS OF SPECIAL COMMITTEES APPOINTED BY THE LAST OR A PRECEEDING COUNCIL

    General report of the work of the year . 5
    Publication of magazine 5
    Invitation to the Presbyterian Church of Canada 5
    Ministerial relief 6

  4 NEW BUSINESS

    Resolution extending greetings of the Council to the United States Minister . 6
    Church Building Association . . . 7
    Minutes memorial of Dr. Alexander and Mrs. Drennan 9

Publication of Council Bulletin . . .	10
Japanese Language School for missionaries. Account of work among foreign residents in Kobe and appointment of a committee to express the sympathy of the Council with the Union Churches in Kobe Yokohama and Tokyo	11
Omission of Proceedings of Devotional Conference from Annual Report, and restriction of Report to one hundred pages	11
Appointment of officers and committees for the ensuing year	11
Preparation of an order of business for the Council, and arrangement for Sunday services held in connection with meetings of Council	12
Sermon of President	12
Publication of papers read at the Devotional Conference.	12
Thanks of the Council to the Committee in charge of the Arima Church . . .	12
Reading and adoption of the minutes; place and date of the next meeting of the Council	12

II GENERAL REPORT OF THE WORK OF THE YEAR

INTRODUCTION	13
EVANGELISTIC WORK	14
EDUCATIONAL WORK	51

	CONCLUSION	71
III	STATISTICAL TABLES	72
IV	PRIVILEGES OBTAINED BY MEIJI GAKUIN, AOYAMA GAKUIN, TOHOKU GAKUIN, AND DOSHISHA . . .	84
V	BOARD OF MISSIONS OF THE CHURCH OF CHRIST IN JAPAN (DENDO KYOKU)	90
VI	ROLL OF THE COUNCIL. .	95

> EAST JAPAN MISSION OF THE PRESBYTERIAN CHURCH IN THE U. S. A. (NORTHERN).
> WEST JAPAN MISSION OF THE PRESBYTERIAN CHURCH IN THE U. S. A. (NORTHERN).
> NORTH JAPAN MISSION OF THE REFORMED (Dutch) CHURCH IN AMERICA.
> SOUTH JAPAN MISSION OF THE REFORMED (Dutch) CHURCH IN AMERICA.
> MISSION OF THE PRESBYTERIAN CHURCH IN THE U. S. (SOUTHERN).
> MISSION OF THE REFORMED (GERMAN) CHURCH IN THE U. S.
> MISSION OF THE CUMBERLAND PRESBYTERIAN CHURCH.
> WOMANS UNION MISSIONARY SOCIETY.

I
PROCEEDINGS
OF THE
TWENTY-SIXTH ANNUAL MEETING OF THE COUNCIL

I OPENING AND SESSIONS OF THE COUNCIL

The Council of Missions Coöperating with the Church Christ in Japan assembled in Arima at 10 a.m., on :ptember 2nd, 1903. The President, the Rev. Henry out, D.D., preached the opening sermon, taking for his xt, *My word shall not return unto me void, but it all accomplish that which I please. Is. 55: 11.*

The roll-call showed an attendance of fifty-four members. 1e Rev. and Mrs. Edward A. Wicher of Kobe and the ev. and Mrs. A. L. Warushuys of Amoy were elected irresponding members.

The morning sessions were preceded by a prayer-eeting from 9 to 9.30. The Devotional Conference was ld on Friday, and the Council adjourned on Saturday,

The following report of the Publications Committee was adopted.

The twenty-fifth Annual Report of the Council wa printed and distributed in the usual manner.

The following have been published by members of th Council :—As hitherto, *Yorokobi no Otozure* and *Chiisak Otozure*, Mrs. E. R. Miller ; *Yakō*, Mr. Jones ; *Fukui Geppō*, Mr. Brokaw ; and *Tohoku Kyokwai Jihō* by member of the Reformed (German) Mission. Dr. Thompson ha printed a second edition of his catechism on the Confessio of Faith of the Church of Christ in Japan ; and th following new tracts in Japanese have been published b Dr. Imbrie : The Living Christ, Master who did sin Eternal Life, In Remembrance of me, Men ough always to pray, Grace and Peace, A great rule and great truth. An English edition of Dr. Lange's Textboo of Colloquial Japanese has been published by Mr. Noss.

The following report of the Committee on Sunday school Literature, presented by Mr. Landis, was adop ed.

The Sunday-school Lesson Helps have been publishe as hitherto in conjunction with the Methodists, Congre gationalists and Baptists. The number of copies printe and the prices are as follows : Primary Leaflet, 8000 a at 12 *sen ;* Scholars Quarterly, 2000 at 25 *sen ;* Teacher Monthly, 1100 at 40 *sen.* The marked increase in th number of copies of the Teachers Monthly taken argue well for an intelligent interest on the part of the teacher: The financial deficit has been reduced from *yen* 1200 t *yen* 850 (in round numbers), or from 25 to 30 per cen This also indicates progress in the right direction.

The Council statistics of the past year show a gain i

---

* Messrs. Imbrie, E. Rothesay Miller, Wyckoff, McIlwaine, MacNa A. D. Hail, H. K. Miller.

Sunday-school members of 1811 in a total of 10226, or 21½ per cent over the figure of the previous year; the previous year showed a gain of 35 per cent over the year 1900; i.e. there has been a gain of 4018 members, or 65 per cent in two years. These figures are encouraging even if in part due to more accurate statistics. They may also be taken as justifying the attention bestowed upon, and the expense incurred in, the publication of the Helps. Such Helps ought certainly to encourage an intelligent interest in Sunday-school work and Bible study. We should as missionaries be forward in the effort to extend their circulation and to enlist our Japanese friends in an intelligent use of them. Teachers' meetings and normal classes ought to be a concern of many more than they are.

A study of the proportion of Sunday-school members to adult church membership will show the backwardness of the Tokyo and Naniwa Presbyteries on this point of Sunday-schools. Even yet the Sunday-school membership of the whole Church lags slightly behind the adult church membership; while two years ago statistics of the Methodist Churches showed their Sunday-school membership to be almost double their church membership. Such facts should make us pause and weigh our opportunities. Perhaps the Council might even call the attention of the Synod or Presbyteries to the great need of still further progress where progress has been so marked the past few years.

Now that the Union Church Hymnal is so soon to be before the various Churches participating, would it not be worth while to inquire whether a similarly ambitious Sunday-school Hymnal is not a great desideratum. Christian Sunday-schools had the honor till lately of leading the children of the empire in music. But late reports state that the secular school is beginning to claim this distinction for itself both in the quality of music and its execution by the children. Surely we cannot easily afford to be deprived of this proud and graceful distinction of the past.

In connection with the consideration of the report on Sunday-school Literature the following resolutions were adopted :—

1 That members of the Council be urged to regard Sunday-schools carried on by them as a part of the regular church work ; and to endeavor to have them included in the statistics furnished by the churches to the Presbyteries.

2 That the Committee on Statistics be requested to pay special attention to the Sunday-school statistics for next year, inquiring how far Sunday-school work carried on by individuals fails to appear in the Presbytery reports ; in case such failure is discovered to be considerable, that the Committee be requested to endeavor to have such work included in the reports ; and, if such endeavor prove unavailing, to report to the next Council the extent to which the Prebytery reports fail to exhibit the entire amount of Sunday-school work done.

3 That the Council request the Standing Committee of Coöperating Christian Missions in Japan to consider the desirability of publishing a Union Sunday-school Hymnal.

The report of the Committee on Statistics,* prepared by Mr. Landis, was read by Mr. Winn and adopted. (For the tables compiled and also for the financial report of the Board of Home Missions of the Church of Christ in Japan, likewise prepared by Mr. Landis, see III and IV following the Proceedings of the Council).

The Treasurers Report for the year was referred to an Auditing Committee,‡ and on the report of the committee was adopted. In view of an expected decrease in the

---

* Messrs. Landis, Winn, Pieters, Myers, Noss, Brokaw.
‡ Messrs. Price and Pieters.

expenses for next year the assessment upon the missions composing the Council was reduced to four *yen* per member.

3 REPORTS OF SPECIAL COMMITTEES APPOINTED BY THE LAST (OR A PRECEDING) COUNCIL.

The General Report of the Work of the Year (see II following Proceedings of the Council) was read by the Rev. H. V. S. Peeke. A resolution was adopted thanking Mr. Peeke and directing that a thousand copies of the report be printed.

The committee* appointed to correspond with the missions regarding the publication of a magazine under the auspices of the Council presented a report containing a summary of the replies received; and, in view of the support guaranteed by the several missions, recommending that the publication of such a magazine be undertaken during the autumn of this year. The following resolution was thereupon adopted :—

That the Rev. E. Rothesay Miller be elected editor in chief; and that two associate editors be elected, one from the Meiji Gakuin and one from Tohoku Gakuin, to serve for one year.

Drs. Imbrie and Sasao, were chosen associate editors.

A letter from the Board of Foreign Missions of the Presbyterian Church of Canada, in response to the invitation of the Council to undertake work in Japan, was read. The reply was to the effect that the Board regards its Formosa field as in Japan, and feels itself unable to extend its operations to other parts of the empire.

---

* Messrs. E. Rothesay Miller, Imbrie, and S. P. Fulton.

The Committee on Ministerial Relief reported as follows :—

In accordance with the request of the Council, all the missions have take action on the plan submitted, and have communicated the same to your committee. The following is a summary of the replies received :—Two missions, the (German) Reformed and the South Japan (Dutch) Reformed, are definitely opposed to any union plan of relief. Two others, the Cumberland Presbyterian and West Japan Presbyterian, are equally definite in favor of a union plan ; though the latter mission desires certain changes in the plan proposed. The other three missions manifest no great interest either way ; but at least leave the way open for further negotiations. One of these, the North Japan (Dutch) Reformed Mission expresses a preference for the plan presented by Mrs. MacNair.

As the plan proposed requires the consent of only three missions, and as two have already pronounced in its favor, it seems probable that a careful revision would gain the assent of at least one more, and thus enable the Council to submit it to the test of actual experience.

A committee of five, consisting of Dr. Wyckoff, Mr. Pieters, Mr. Winn, Dr. A. D. Hail and Mr. Lampe, was appointed to revise the plan in the light of the suggestions offered by the West Japan Presbyterian Mission and to send it in its new form to the missions favoring a union plan, together with the following questions :—

1 Do you approve the plan as now presented ; and will you join in the establishment of such a fund ?
2 If you approve of the general idea but desire changes in details, will you appoint a committee to confer with similar committees from other missions also approving ?

4   NEW BUSINESS

A resolution was adopted extending the cordial

greetings of the Council to the Hon. Lloyd C. Griscom, Minister of the United States to Japan; wishing him full success in the discharge of his many responsibilities; and assuring him of its constant interest and prayers.

A plan for the organization of a Church Building Association was presented by Mr. Price and others; and after slight amendment was adopted as follows :—

PRESBYTERIAN CHURCH BUILDING ASSOCIATION

ARTICLE I   OBJECT

The object of this Association shall be to assist in providing suitable houses of worship for the Christians of the Nihon Kirisuto Kyokwai (Church of Christ in Japan).

ARTICLE II   ORGANIZATION

1   Any person or organization in sympathy with the purpose of the Association and taking at least one share in it shall be enrolled as a member.
2   The business of the Association shall be transacted by a Board of Directors. A quorum shall consist of four members of the Board.
3   The Board of Directors shall consist of six missionaries (men) connected with the Council of Missions, one of whom shall act as Secretary and Treasurer.
4   The Board of Directors shall be elected by a majority vote of the Council of Missions Coöperating with the Nihon Kirisuto Kyokwai. The term of office of a member of the Board of Directors shall be three years. In electing the first Board the Council shall determine which members shall retire after the first and which after the second year.
5   In case vacancies occur, the Board of Directors shall elect men to fill them until the next meeting of the Council.
6   The Board of Directors shall present an Annual

Report to the Council, and all matters of business calling for consideration shall be discussed. The Association shall hold no general meetings.

7 The Association shall be considered as established when as many as fifty shares have been taken.

ARTICLE III INCOME

1 The source of income shall be by equal assessments on the shares of the Association. Every application for membership shall state how many shares will be taken.

2 No one assessment shall be for more than two *yen* per share.

3 The total of assessments for one year shall not be greater than ten *yen* per share.

4 All moneys received from assessments shall be given to the bodies of Christians needing assistance. Every share shall pay the sum of thirty *sen* per annum for administration expenses.

ARTICLE IV DISBURSEMENT OF FUNDS

1 No grant in aid for a place of worship shall be made without a formal application being presented to the Board of Directors.

In every case the missionary interested in that special field or residing nearest to it shall be consulted.

2 Each application shall state the approximate cost of building and land (if land is to be bought), and the amount in aid desired. In no case, however, shall a grant in aid exceed one-third of the estimated outlay. Nor shall such grant be made until at least one-third of the entire amount to be expended has actually been raised by the applicants. Each application shall also state how the balance of the money is to be raised and in what way the property is to be held.

3 After the Board of Directors has decided upon the amount to be given to any the particular church, the Secretary shall send out a notice to all the members, giving

the name of the place where church is to be built and the amount of the assessment. (See ART. III, SEC. 2.)

ARTICLE V   OFFICERS

1   The Secretary and Treasurer shall be elected by the Board of Directors.
2   The Secretary shall keep a record of all the meetings of the Board of Directors, and of all applications for aid.
3   The Treasurer shall receive and disburse all funds.

ARTICLE VI   AMENDMENTS

Amendments to this Constitution may be submitted to the Council of Missions at any regular meeting of the Council. If a two-thirds vote of the members of Council present is cast in favor of the amendment it shall considered carried. No amendment shall be acted upon on the day of its presentation.

The following were elected Directors of the Church Building Association: For three years, Messrs. Price and Pieters; for two years, Messrs. Winn and A. D. Hail; for one year, Messrs. G. W. Fulton and McAlpine.

Dr. A. D. Hail and the Rev. T. C. Winn were appointed a committee to prepare minutes memorial of Dr. T. T. Alexander and Mrs. A. M. Drennan. The following were presented and adopted:—

The Rev. T. T. Alexander D.D., one of the oldest members of this Council, died at Honolulu, on Nov. 14th, 1902. In his decease the Council has lost a member who was a most devoted servant of Christ, and whose labors were very varied and successful; and it hereby places on record its high appreciation of his life and service as a missionary, and its great sorrow at losing him from its counsels and from a share in the work of the Church of Christ in Japan. To Mrs. Alexander and her children the Council expresses genuine sympathy in their affliction, commending them to the God of the widow and the fatherless for his gracious care and comfort. It also extends its sympathy to the Japan Missions and to the Board of Foreign Missions of the Presbyterian Church in the U. S. A.

Mrs. A. M. Drennan of the Japan Mission of the Cumberland Presbyterian Church, who entered into her rest June. 26th, 1903, began her work in Japan in May 1883. Her missionary life and labors thus span a score of the best years of her life. These years of effort and endeavor she gave lovingly and unstintingly to the work of her Lord. Her home was always open to the calls of the work and to the demands of Christian hospitality. The first years of her missionary service were spent in connection with the founding of the Wilmina Girls School of Osaka; and her final years in the City of Tsu in the Province of Ise, where for a number of years she was the only resident missionary, and where she was permitted to see the organization of the church in that place. The Council herewith expresses its high appreciation of her personal worth and of her work, and extends its sympathy to her bereaved friends, to her mission and to the Board of Missions of the Cumberland Presbyterian Church.

The following resolutions were adopted :—

Whereas the Council is convinced that a small monthly publication in English would prove a valuable means of communication, of disseminating information, and of increasing interest among friends in America, resolved:

1 That Mr. Cameron Johnson, an Associate Member of the Southern Presbyterian Mission, be requested to undertake the work of editing and publishing such a monthly to be called the Council Bulletin.

2 That a committee consisting of Mr. McAlpine, Mr.

Lathom and Dr. Langsdorf be appointed to assist Mr. Johnson in establishing the Bulletin.

3 That in case Mr. Johnson accept this invitation he be authorized to draw on the Treasurer of the Council for funds not to exceed fifty *yen* for the first year.

4 That in case such a monthly can not be established without greater financial assistance from the Council, the committee be requested to prepare a suitable plan and present it at the next meeting of the Council.

The following resolution was adopted :—

Whereas in many places the difficulties connected with the acquisition of a practical knowledge of the Japanese language are very great, resolved :
That the Council request the Standing Committee of Coöperating Christian Missions to take steps for the establishment of a central Language School at some suitable place.

The Rev. Edward A. Wicher addressed the Council regarding his work among the foreigners residing in Kobe; and Messrs. Price and Winn were appointed a committee to convey to the Union Churches in Kobe Yokohama and Tokyo an expression of sympathy on the part of the Council and assurance of remembrance in its prayers.

A resolution was adopted that the Proceedings of the Devotional Conference be omitted from the Annual Report of the Council, and that endeavor be made to restrict the Report as printed to one hundred pages.

The following officers were appointed to serve during the ensuing year: President, Dr. D. B. Schneder; Vice President, Mr. George P. Pierson; Secretary, Mr. H. W. Myers; Treasurer, John C. Ballagh, Esq.

The following committees were appointed:—

Publications: Drs. Imbrie, Oltmans, S. P. Fulton, A. D. Hail, and Moore.

Statistics: Mr. Landis, Dr. Murray, Messrs. Faust, Harris, Logan, and Peeke.

Program for Devotional Conference: Messrs. Curtis, W. C. Buchanan, and Lampe.

Arrangements and entertainment: Mr. Price and Dr. A. D. Hail.

The officers of the Council were requested to prepare an order of business and to report to the next meeting of the Council; and also, during the year, to invite members of the Council or others to conduct the Sunday services held at the time of the annual meeting of the Council.

Dr. Stout was requested to send his sermon to the editor of the Fukuin Shimpō for publication.

The writers of the papers read at the Devotional Conference were requested to send them for publication to the Japan Evangelist; and, with such revision as may be necessary, to the Fukuin Shimpō.

The Council extended its thanks to the committee in charge of the Arima Church for the use of the building and other courtesies.

The Minutes were read and adopted; and the Council adjourned with prayer to meet in Arima, on July 16th 1904, at 8 p.m.

II
GENERAL REPORT OF THE WORK OF THE YEAR

BY THE

Rev. H. V. S. PEEKE

Fortunate is the man who is called upon to prepare the Annual Report of the Council at a time in regard to which one of our oldest missionaries* can say, "The people are more easily approached and affected with the gospel than they have ever been since the country was first opened"; and when a missioanary just added to our number† can say, "Things look very encouraging to me, and I feel that the people are very eager for the word of God"; while one who stands midway between them‡ says, "I think the work in the Hokurikudō is in a better condition than it has been in fourteen years at least. We find that the people are not only willing to hear, but more willing to receive Christianity than formerly."

This is the unanimous testimony from the Hokkaidō to Kyūshū. One brother, just returned from furlough,§ says that the change is not all that the reports of Taikyo

---

* Dr. David Thompscn. † Mr. Stick. ‡ Mr. G. W. Fulton. § Dr. J, P. Moore.

Dendō had led him to expect; but "yet there is a change for the better. There is new life, and the prospects in evangelistic work have indeed greatly improved." The number of persons baptized is of course large. One missionary speaks of baptizing fifty-seven, another over fifty, and still another seventy-nine. Many missionaries have baptized more persons during this last year than during any previous year of their service.

In our educational work it is the same. Many of the schools are full to over-flowing. The grade of instruction, the quality of teachers and the spiritual life of the student body, is better than ever before. To be sure, all things are not what we wish and hope and pray for, but the simple tale of mission prosperity and fullness of opportunity along all lines is such that one is almost bound to doubt the sober judgment of the chronicler.

This year of prosperity has its special lessons for us just as had the years of leanness and adversity, and I trust that each of us may have a mind to search these out and learn. We will consider the evangelistic work first, as being the real heart of all our operations; and I will ask you to take the editor's standpoint, and consider it from Kyūshū to the Hokkaidō.

EVANGELISTIC WORK

Kyūshū reports prosperity just as far as work is done. The only limit seems to be in the number of workers available. Distress on this account has become more acute of late, and the painful point has been reached where important out-stations will have to be abandoned for lack of workers. At this time of greatest opportunity, of greatest promise, the force is weaker than ever before.

Still, the people are cordial, and are gradually entering the Church. The number of Christian teachers in Middle and Normal schools is already astonishing, and there are also a few Christians even among Primary School teachers. Being a Christian is less and less of an obstacle to obtaining employment. The graduates of mission schools are a help in many ways. In some places they are the chief workers in the church.

The only missionaries in this field are those of the Reformed Church in America, though the West Presbyterian Mission has out-stations on the island. The field is too broad for them. They cannot properly work more than half of it, and have besought the West Japan Mission and the Southern Presbyterian Mission to locate families in the north and north-east of the island. It is painful to contemplate the prospects of this most promising and important field, if after having done their best their efforts are not soon supplemented by other missions.

Crossing the straits at Shimo-no-seki, we do not find the missionaries in Sanyō as enthusiastic as those in some other parts. They too feel the fewness and inadequacy of the working force, and mourn over the indifference of many; but they also bear witness to readiness to listen, greater willingness to enter preaching places and the openness of the homes. They refer to a growing feeling of responsibility for evangelistic work felt by believers. In some parts of the country a lack of this feeling is deplored; but on the whole it is evident that the Japanese Christians feel, as they never have before, that it is theirs, not the missionary's work. Buddhist opposition is not what it once was. In most places it is *nil*. And even the general callousness of Buddhist believers seems to be gradually softening.

There is a gap in our missionary forces at Okayama. That is a Congregational strong-hold; but just as these brethren have thought it wise to open work in Nagasaki and Hakodate in recent years, so we would do well to strengthen our work in the Okayama region by locating a missionary family. It is a comfort to learn of the success attending the aggressive operations put forth in Kyōto and Kōbe. These fields are but comparatively recently occupied, but still are very successful.

Right here it is well to speak of what has been, no doubt a great factor in their success: viz. the greater readiness of the people to carry their religion from place to place. A few years ago it was very common for people to move and not make a new church alliance for months, perhaps not at all. Now that is the exception; but there is a great leak yet. This was referred to by some of your number; and Mr. Van Dyke writes strongly on the subject in the Report of the Standing Committee. Still we have much on this score for which to rejoice.

The same tale of prosperity comes from the Hokurikudō. At Fukui there has been Buddhist activity. Even open *kōgisho* preaching is indulged in; but no special opposition and the people are more friendly. One cannot but feel that our body is weak farther up that coast. Ought we not to have missionaries stationed in Toyama or Niigata?

Work is being prosecuted actively on Shikoku at every point. It is the old tale of unbounded opportunity. We have missionaries in each of the four *ken* and have reason to be fairly satisfied with our prospects.

The Cumberland Presbyterian Mission is hampered by lack of evangelists; but is to be congratulated that in these prosperous times it has an unusually full complement of missionaries, excepting single lady evangelists residing out of Osaka. They seem to cover chosen territory well, and report persistent village work. Indeed this is a pleasant feature, not only of their report, but of that of some others. For instance, near Matsuyama in Iyo, eighteen were baptized in a village of 600 houses. It will be years before some of us can do much for the smaller places, but it is a happy thing that some are able to effectively prosecute this branch of work.

Passing on up to the Tōkyō region and that cared for by the missionaries residing in that city, we find the same general encouragements; but at the same time a tone of sadness caused by the contracted condition of the work. Out-stations sadly neglected, others abandoned, a shortness of workers even for organized churches, even some self-supporting ones. This must needs make the hearts of the missionaries heavy. Careful husbandry yields a hundred-fold; but where are the reapers?

The (German) Reformed work centering at Sendai is compact, well organized, well manned and aggressive. The mission doubtless feels limitations similar to the rest us; yet its publications and reports give the impression that it has the men, the right kind of men, Japanese and foreign, and the money too. In fact, it is planning to branch out into the Hokkaidō; a fact that cannot but cause rejoicing in the hearts of the widely scattered workers there.

The reports of the missionaries at Morioka and Aomori lend no variation to the tale of unlimited opportunity and open doors. Speaking of calling at the homes of Sunday-school children, Mr. Harris says, " One who is cheerful, buoyant and courageous will find the door of these homes ever open." This is true at present for nearly the whole country.

Coming to the Hokkaidō, we simply succumb to the inevitable, and put in Mr. Pierson's report bodily. " In the Hokkaidō the past year marks a distinct advance towards the acceptance of the gospel as the religion for the empire and the religion for the individual. Things are getting serious in Japan. A well known literary man, Mr. Nakae, sees no solution of the mystery of life; and, knowing his days are numbered, writes a book which begins with matter and ends with despair. A former Hokkaidō student seeks in vain for certainty in the maze of unchristian philosophy and religions (from which Japan in happily emerging) and casts away his life in a Nikkō waterfall, with no hope; because with no God in the world.

But where one of Mr. Nakae's books is read, two of Mr. Takahashi Goro's Christian answer are read. The student's suicide has quickened the public mind to a more earnest quest of the truth. The most popular book among educated people to-day, is Mr. Kuroiwa's, " What is Human Life?" Mr. Kuroiwa is the editor of a large Tōkyō newspaper. His book leads up to the Christian solution. There is more than one voice in the wilderness preparing the way of the Lord. These are interesting and happy days in mission work in Japan.

Last year in the Hokkaido the crops were short and the fisheries below the average, and the famine of North Hondō was felt more or less in South Hokkaido; but it was a good year spiritually. Any and every year is a strategic year with us. It is more important to influence a *making* age than *disintegrating* age. In old Japan there is a dissolution of old faiths going on. In the Hokkaido every cluster of thatched huts in the clearing in the wilderness is full of promise and full of peril. It is dreadfully lonely, the stumps, the malaria, the mud and the bears; but you pass on a little and see the more advanced farms and the new towns, and you conclude that Japan has a treasure island here whose hidden wealth she has only begun to uncover. The new age, the freedom of a new country, and the new spirit of progress, are all helps to the Christian preacher. As was said last year, and the year before that, and still the year before that, and as will likely be said next year, NOW is the time for the evangelization of the Hokkaidō."

Now, as to the cause of this change in sentiment toward Christianity so manifest everywhere, it is hardly the province of your editor to philosophize. He would only say that it seems to have had its beginning, or at least it seems to have become specially evident, toward the close of last year.

Lest it be thought that we have over-colored matters in this review of the evangelistic field, let us in our own defense make a few quotations.

From Morioka,* "The fields are indeed white to the harvest, and doors and avenues for work are opening faster than we are able to enter. Angels might well envy us the many opportunities which are coming to us." From Yokohama,† "There is a widespread spirit of inquiry, or readiness to hear faithful gospel preaching. I

---

* Miss Winn. † Mr. Jas. H Ballagh.

was struck with this in my own daily meetings in the early part of the year, in the attendance and earnestness, and readiness to embrace spiritual truth and profess faith in Christ. The same may be said of places where there have been no special efforts put forth, or even stated workers or preachers of the gospel." From Osaka,* " While in our work during the year, as a whole, there have been hindrances enough to keep us humble, discouragements enough to keep down all Utopian anticipations, and opposition enough to tone down unhealthy optimism, yet in looking back over it all, in no one year has the work of the mission shown more substantial results than the past year. This is true in regard to the growth of the churches in numbers and efficiency of organization, in the spirit of self-support and general Christian enterprise, and in the development of our girls-school work."

I should next like to call your attention to various opinions in regard to special phases of evangelistic work that have come out in the reports.

LACK OF EVANGELISTS :—This is felt from one end of the country to the other, but seems to be more acute the farther south one goes. Not so much is said about it by missionaries north of Tōkyō. It is a state of affairs that tries men's souls, and is hard on our ambitions either purely religious or denominational. At the same time there are compensations. The missionary is saved from the danger of lording it over God's heritage ; he knows better, and more thoroughly sympathizes with, the few men associated with him. It opens his eyes as nothing else could to the fact that godly evangelists are above all things the product of the Spirit's work only. Men of sufficient education and sufficient piety to teach satisfactorily in mission schools can be found with comparative ease ; but men of the knowledge and devotion necessary to meet the high requirements of the evangelist's office are hard to find, and hard to raise up. The Spirit's work

* Dr. A. D. Hail.

must necessarily precede all other preparation. Men called of the Spirit are the men we must have.

Yet some men are coming forward. Five Kyūshū young men are now in preparation. From Osaka* comes the word that, "Since the Day of Prayer for Colleges, and the united prayer that God would send more workers into his harvest there has been an encouraging increase in the number of those who are willing to give themselves to the work of the ministry." Is not the Lord waiting the time when we shall all be driven to our knees in utter dependence upon his Spirit rather than on our machinery, with the purpose of then blessing us with a truly consecrated body of preachers?

A Kyūshū correspondent† thinks that the Church and the ministry are unconcerned over this matter, but it is hardly probable that this is true for the whole country. It is true, however, that there is little hope for improvement until the Japanese Christians and evangelists as well as the missionaries are acutely distressed over the present lack, and implore the Lord of the harvest to supply it. Most important is it that we do not become stampeded, and make the mistake of filling our ranks with uncalled or untrained men.

SELF-SUPPORT :—It is evident that there has been no striking advance along the line of self support, but steady progress has not been lacking. It is becoming thoroughly understood throughout the Church at large, that believers are to contribute to the support of the work, and there is no indication of a tendency to shirk this. The problem is to choose and carry out a good system of finance during the period that a large part of the support comes from the missions. There is no doubt that the people do better for some benevolent object, or for some special enterprise than they do for their regular church expenses; but that is perfectly natural, and is universal. The envelope system is in quite general use, and well suited to the country. Its success depends on getting a contribu-

---

* Dr. A. D. Hail.   † Mr. Pieters.

tion from every one, present or absent; and that requires a faithful and enthusiastic deacon, with proper assistants. Much has been gained when a system has been adopted and finances can be talked about without embarrassment. Some regard tithing as a solvent for much of the financial problem. The Osaka East Church has a number of tithers, and has entered the ranks of the thousand dollar churches. It averages Yen 9.26 per member; the lowest average spoken of in the same connection is Yen 1.74 per member.

It may be helpful in some cases to consider the local contributions as a whole, reckoning a work as self-supporting during three or four months of the year, and letting the Christians feel the weight of responsibility during that length of time. This is such an important matter that the Council should at some time have a special report on it. The Moji Church had a legacy left it by a godly woman. This is certainly a rare occurrence. One cannot but regret that the interest of this fund is to be applied to pastoral support. Unless great care is taken, such funds become millstones around the neck of spirituality.

It is pleasant to note that, on the whole, the active canvass for funds for the Board of Missions (Dendo Kyoku) does not act as a hindrance to local finances. A well milked udder gives but the more. The business-like methods of the Board make the financial problem a dignified one, and takes away the well-bred distaste for discussing money matters which was the legacy of *Bushido*. One* has well said that if the Dendō Kyoku draws away from the support of local work, it rather indicates some fault in the methods of the church or mission.

The following is pertinent:§ "Being in connection here with the work of the Dendō Kyoku, I have been impressed with the fact that there is little or no difference between the methods of this body and those current among

---

* Dr. Haworth. § Mr. Pieters.

the missions of the Council. I expected to find more difference. Of course the efficiency of these methods depends largely upon the man employed. In choosing such men the Dendō Kyoku is much freer than the missions are; and consequently ought to get, and probably does get, on the average, better men. An invitation to work for the Dendō Kyoku has three advantages which the mission does not offer: (1) Higher salaries; (2) working for their own people; (3) ordination. For it seems to be the plan of the Dendō Kyoku to secure the ordination of every man that comes into its employ. In regard to this latter point, it seems to me that the principles upon which men are to be ordained should be more clearly fixed in the Church than they are. I think the believers under the Dendō Kyoku do better in the matter of self-support than those who receive assistance from the missions. This is largely to be accounted for from the fact that they are so much closer to the source of supply. They are constantly being appealed to for contributions, and see the appeal made to their fellow believers of the Nihon Kirisuto Kyōkwai. They read, month by month, the reports of the treasury; and feel, when the Dendō Kyoku is in straits, that they ought to strain every nerve to help themselves. It is impossible to give believers who are assisted by the missions quite the same feeling. The foreign boards are so far away, their operations are so indistinct and they are relatively so powerful, that it seems to make but little difference whether they contribute or not. Moreover, the same boards spend large sums of money upon missionaries' salaries and other luxuries, the usefulness of which is not apparent to the ordinary Japanese believer. To some extent, I am convinced we missionaries may, and ought to overcome these difficulties by explaining matters to the Japanese and keeping the subject before them; but in the nature of the case we cannot do so well as the Dendō Kyoku; and the practice of turning over work to that body when it has reached an advanced stage, seems to be a wise one."

We all wish to develop our work; to increase the

number of our out-stations. But however many good evangelists may be available, there must be money to support them. This must come either from the Dendō Kyoku, i.e. indirectly, through their taking off our hands work well along toward self-support; from American Christians contributing through the usual channels in increased quantity; or from the Japanese Christians, through their individually contributing more generously and unfailingly to the support of the local work, thus relieving mission funds for expansion.

There is little to hoped for from the first source; for the Dendō Kyoku's chief cares will generally lie without our bounds. Some of us feel that we are gradually approaching the limit of the funds for evangelistic work that we can hope to get from America. Our hope for development really lies in leading the Christians to a great assumption of the support of their evangelists; and the sooner we realize this and act on it, the better. A *yen* or so of increase yearly at each point counts for a good deal in the aggregate. We must study ways of showing our Japanese brethren that our work depends, yes, depends a great deal, on each one of them contributing his quota. It is proposed to rely for the expansion of Japanese state railroads upon the profits of the lines already built. It is a sound proposition. Ninomiya Sontoku, Japan's great economist, enunciated the principle that from the profits of newly cleared and cultivated fields must new fields be brought under cultivation. This principle must in some way or other find its place in our structure of self-support.

BUILDING OPERATIONS:—There is much that is gratifying to report in regard to building. To touch on that which is purely missionary, we note a new dormitory and recitation hall at the girls-school in Sendai. The mission has also put up an office. A new chapel is going up at the Meiji Gakuin. A new building has been erected for the girls-school at Sapporo. Coming to churches, we find new buildings at Kyōto, Okazaki, Toyama and Gifu; a parsonage also at the latter place. Church erection is being reduced to a science at Kobe. There is a settled conviction on the part of missionaries and Japanese that it is necessary to buy a lot and put up a building at the earliest possible moment. It is a most paying investment financially and spiritually. The Christians take to the idea heartily, and there has been a boom this year in beginning funds for church erection. There is probably hardly a Christian community of considerable size in any part of the country without its fund, if it has no building. Tokushima has refurnished its church with benches, which are reported as "the most comfortable I've seen anywhere in Japan." It is refreshing to learn that there are benches thought comfortable in even one church in the empire. We trust a pattern will be furnished to all askers, and that many will ask.

This is from the Hokkaidō*: "At Mororan the Christians have purchased the lot next the church for a pastor's house. At Piuka they have money and labor and timber for a new church. At Asahigawa we hope to build a thousand dollar church this summer. At Bie the town gave us a lot and promises a hundred *yen* if we will furnish the other hundred. To secure the land we must promise a building of certain dimensions within a certain time." The fine lot for the Asahigawa church worth 600 *yen*, was the generous gift of one member of the congregation.

The (German) Reformed missionaries are making a special move in this direction.† One of them urges building; and emphasizes the wisdom of buying, not renting, the lot. It is well too to make sure of a lot large enough not only for present purposes, but within wise limits for expected future expansion. A lot of a hundred *tsubo*, if of the right shape, will answer for a small church and parsonage at present, and a good large church later on; while a narrow lot, however long, soon reaches its limitations as a church site.

The Nihon Kirisuto Kyōkwai has fallen behind in the

---

* Mr. Pierson.   † Mr. H. K. Miller.

matter of church buildings. Father Okuno was specially impressed with this on his recent tour. Now is the time to supply the lack, for the people have an undoubted interest in the subject.

The following in regard to the Kyōto church is so instructive that it must find a place in this report.* " The church is one of the most beautiful and well built that I have seen in Japan. It is 48 ft. by 36; and with a small gallery at the rear will accommodate about 300 people. The cost of the building was about 1400 *yen*. Of this more than half came from purely Japanese sources. Not more than a half a dozen of the Christians are at all well to do. The secret of their generous giving lies in this, that the people had a mind to work and deny themselves. Just after it was decided to build, the women formed a *Shigotokwai* (work society), and by their diligence succeeded in raising 70 *yen*. For the most part this was the result of their needle-work. One woman, the wife of our Kyōto evangelist, with three small children and no servant, coached a boy in English to enter the Commercial School, and contributed the proceeds to this fund. The boys of the Endeavor Society, by distributing notices of religious meetings, running errands, twisting gold thread, etc., earned ten *yen*. The girls of the society, by sewing and knitting, raised twenty-three *yen*. The Sunday-school of little girls, which is held in the kindergarten building in the weaving district, contributed ten *yen*. Last, but not least, the One Rin Society gave ninety *yen*. I must add a word as to this society. About ten years ago, a handful of women in the church agreed to lay aside one *rin* a day for the Lord. And now when the time came for using this fund, it was found that their offerings had amounted to *ninety thousand rin*.

BIBLE CLASSES :—It has been a delight to record the amount of Bible instruction carried on. A good deal of this is done in English it is true, a thing to be regretted ; but since much of it would be impossible were

---

* Mr. Curtis.

it not for the English, let us rather simply rejoice that it is done. It would seem that there is hardly a missionary, man or woman. married or single, that does not each week face at least one class, in many cases several classes, in the Bible. The pupils are mostly students ; though prison officials, post office officials, and army officers also occupy the benches. The students are drawn from every kind of school. Teachers and pupils often study together. Teachers often act as interpreters, and often organize the classes. Teaching is done in missionaries' homes, in student boarding houses, and in some cases actually in the school buildings themselves after hours.* Some of these classes live but a few weeks and their membership is very evanescent. Others run along for months, their members come to church services, and finally unite with the Church.

The following is the way the matter has worked out in Ashigawa. "We were forced to begin English Bible class work will-nilly by the youth athirst for learning. But we limited ourselves to two evenings a week, to be English Bible only, and every student *must* attend church or Sunday-school once on Sunday or forfeit his English class on Tuesday and Friday. This plan, rigorously pursued, especially with a band of wild Chu Gakko boys, has worked remarkably well. The boys not only attend Sunday-school, but voluntarily attend our Junior C. E. Society, and actually clamored to have it meet once a week instead of twice a month. The English class, begun with prayer and singing, is in itself a religious meeting; and recently, following on some remarkable revival meetings by Dr. Franson of the Scandinavian Alliance Mission,† twelve of the men were led to confess their sins and plead on their knees to God for forgiveness."‡

It is a practice quite satisfactory to some missionaries to be their own interpreters ; giving the instruction first in English, then in Japanese. This is certainly a good thing if one can do it.

---

* Mr. Price. † Dr. Hail. ‡ Mrs. G. P. Pierson.

There is no question that the attitude of the student and teacher classes toward the missionary and his Bible has undergone a radical change. It is hard to find the cause, but no doubt the presence of many mission school graduates and other Christians among the teachers of the Middle Schools accounts largely for this. It is not unusual for missionaries to be asked to address schools, even Normal Schools,* in sections where this would have been impossible some years ago. In Nagoya† an opportunity was thus given that had been awaited for years. To be sure the missionary does not preach on these occasions, but it a recognition of his character and standing which all counts in the long run. Opposition on the part of teachers is not wanting, and there is ill-will in some quarters; but it is as rare as was good-will in former years. Night schools have been carried on in Kochi and Kobe with good results in the former, and little satisfaction in the latter case. The East Church Osaka rents a house opposite the church and carries on a similar work. The missionary must have some point of social contact with the people, and it is a thing almost impossible to get one with the middle-aged. He can by means of English, and various other lines of instruction, get readily into kindly and intimate relations with the youth. To get into such intimate relations is the first step to leading men to our Saviour; so however much we may in theory be opposed to these so-called indirect methods, it is probably wiser to bow and make use of them. For the fact stands out that not only are a great many being converted by these means to-day, but large numbers of our most trustworthy Christians entered the kingdom through this door. With this purpose of gaining acquaintance and intimacy, a number of other plans are used. There are the knitting classes. Some half dozen report cooking classes. One lady‡ teaches music to Normal School pupils. Really, one wonders what the missionary does not teach, from dress-making to Greek. Provided one has first made him

---
* Mr. E. R. Miller. † Mr. McAlpine. ‡ Mrs. W. Y. Jones.

self competent in the language, it is hard to see why it is not as proper to use these methods of cultivating social relations as it was for the Saviour to go to the wedding in Cana of Galilee.

SUNDAY-SCHOOLS:—It is equally gratifying to record the prosperity of Sunday-school work. Just as with special Bible classes, there is but one voice from north to south. Many mission households mean a Sunday-school for small children; while many have two or three under their care. Attendance runs from a dozen to a hundred. The pupils of girls-schools enlisted in this work are to be counted by the dozens. One of the most encouraging features is that in connection with many of the churches we find organized schools; i.e. schools run on the home plan, with classes, collections, opening and closing exercises, etc. Further, while Sunday-schools were formerly the missionary's special property, the churches are becoming interested in them as their own work and responsibility.

To carry on a good Sunday-school, good teachers are needed; teachers who know, who can teach, and who will be responsible. We hear[*] of the wife of a telegraph operator who comes four miles each Sunday to teach her class. Kanazawa[†] has a weekly teachers meeting and a monthly meeting of all the Sunday-school workers in the city. In Ferris Seminary and other institutions teachers are carefully prepared. The results of such work are bound to be good. It is useless simply to deplore lack of teachers, when proper effort can train them.

There is an indication in many places of a carefully organized main school at the church, with the ordinary schools for children at outside points. At Kagoshima there was a Sunday afternoon meeting of all the schools at the church previous to the summer vacation. It was a great success. One felt that the Sunday-schools had arrived at self-consciousness. The central school alone is

---

[*] Miss S. Alexander. [†] Miss Luther.

to be kept up during the summer; but pupils of the other schools were encouraged to attend, and some do attend. The exercises of the meeting were largely musical; and for a wonder there was no cake.

Good Sunday-schools increase the church attendance, and open many doors for calling. Here, as at home, it is most difficult to make our schools interesting for boys and girls of fourteen or fifteen. Some* have found it a good idea to have the Sunday-school an hour before the evening service. Others† have made the morning gathering for the church people and their children, while another at the same place in the afternoon, has been for the neighborhood. We have been accustomed to hear a great deal about the opposition of primary-school teachers, but that has become almost a negligible factor. In fact they have become our teachers in some schools. We hear‡ of children's meetings conducted on week day evenings. It seems a good plan. In most places the only limit to work of this kind in the strength of the workers. Many speak of pupils uniting with the Church.

Opinions in regard to the Lesson Helps furnished by the Committee are very divided. There are those who think highly of them, feel they could not get along without them, and speak of better attendance since they were introduced. Their use certainly does introduce an element of uniformity in the opening and closing exercises, and tends to increase the *esprit du corps;* but there is some criticism. They are spoken of as too difficult. One worker would prefer a set of lessons on the life of Christ, probably for small children; but this cannot be prepared by the Committee so long as it is restricted to the International Lessons. The Quarterly certainly is pretty difficult for pupils excepting those well on in the Chū Gakkō; and it is too manifestly a translation.

Nothing came in to show how the Monthly is regarded. We are behind some of the missions coöperating with us in our appreciation and use of these helps; § and

---

* Mr. Winn.   † Dr. A. D. Hail.   ‡ Mr. Van Horn.   § Mr. Landis.

in spite of the adverse criticism, it is no doubt to our own loss. At the same time, we record a hope that the helps will be framed more closely to our needs.

One writer* gives a rather severe criticism of Sunday-schools. "In anything I have seen of Sunday-schools for little children thus far, they are very difficult to manage. I do not know of any that have been an unqualified success. Regular attendance is hardly to be counted on. Only the smallest youngsters are to be gotten hold of, with perhaps a few of the larger girls. The boys fight shy. The Christians on the whole do not manifest much interest in the institution either for their own children or for others. Practically all the Sunday-school work is done by the missionaries or their helpers. Few of the Christians are willing to take hold and teach, though they may be qualified to do so. The Sunday-schools of the churches are for adults; really a collection of Bible classes. Preaching-place Sunday-schools vary very much in attendance and deportment, but both are usually of a poor order." Very few missionaries actually engaged in Sunday-school work will recognize this as a picture of the conditions as they have observed them. The same writer adds, "Occasionally, however, there are parents who will bring their children to the door, and then come for them again at the close." Two reports speak of physicians who have taken special pains to enter their children into Sunday-school.

The earnest, evangelistic spirit among the pupils of the girls-schools is very striking. Judging from the reports, the work at Ferris Seminary is unusually well organized and effective. The account† of the main Sunday-school in Morioka is so suggestive that we insert it entire. "'The church Sunday-school is flourishing. Only once since November has the attendance been less than 100; frequently it has been over 150. The school is divided into nine classes, two of which are composed of adults. Our household supplies three of the teachers; the other six are

---

* Mr. G. W. Fulton. † Miss Deyo.

from the Christians of the place. Occasionally the class sits through a lesson period without a teacher, but not often. The uniting of classes without a teacher is not permitted. The school may be said to be modeled on the American plan. The international Leaflet and Quarterly are used for all but the infant class, though I wish we had something simpler and more fundamental for the two primary classes of the first and second *Jinjō* grades. The opening exercises include a good deal of singing, a short drill on the Commandments, or the Creed, Lord's Prayer, or some text containing a doctrinal truth; then comes the division into classes, and on reassembling, the Lesson Story with its teachings is reviewed with the large colored picture from America, and the Golden Text recited. A little text card and a copy of the *Otozure* is given to each child. A collection is taken up in each class in tin boxes—condensed milk tins with new tops soldered on and a slit cut in, to be opened twice a year. The attendance in each class is kept and read publicly before the close of school. The classes are numbered. Many of the older pupils stay to the church services. We are working to get all from the Kōtō grade up to do so."

We cannot close these paragraphs in regard to Sunday-school work without speaking in terms of the very highest praise of the collection of Sunday-school songs edited by Mrs. Jones and Miss Glenn. These songs have been the very life of the Sunday-school work in at least one place (Kagoshima). The work would be sorely handicapped without them. They may strike one as difficult on first acquaintance; but the children learn them readily, and they have a life and movement that is hard to find elsewhere.

BIBLE-WOMEN and WORK FOR WOMEN:—Not as much information on this topic as was expected came to hand. Women's societies exist in many places, and some by means of their handiwork earn money for benevolent purposes or church erection. In others a simple prayer-meeting is held. One writer* prefers the comparatively

---

* Miss Leavitt.

simple *Fujin-kwai* to the organization into a branch of the *Kyōfukwai* with its many departments that was rather forced upon them. An energetic Bible-woman at Kanazawa brings people to meetings, and calls at the home of pupils. A good Bible woman has given new life to Sunday-school work in Okazaki. The school at No. 212 Yokohama has twenty women in training, and a goodly number working two by two.* As to access to the women in their homes, there is apparently nothing left to be desired. A foreigner seems to be welcomed as readily as a Japanese.

A report from Miss Haworth has arrived too late to be largely utilized, but it tells of a great deal of successful endeavor in a social way with the missionary's home as a center. Careful inquiry into the methods of the Kyōto work will well repay the trouble. Six Bible-women are working in connection with Mrs. MacNair, and her report indicates prosperity at every point. There is large attendance at Sunday-schools and "unusual interest among people of mature years." The same thing must be said in regard to the report of Mrs. Pierson. The simple fact is that the members of the Council ought to publish a little monthly sheet in which such inspiriting information as is found in these two and a number of other reports, could go down in full. We are really culpable in not making use of a method whose utility has been proved by Methodists Congregationalists and Baptists. By such a publication we should realize clearly our strength and our responsibility; and by learning of one another's attempts, successes and failures, at the time of their happening, our efficiency would be greatly increased.

SPECIAL EVANGELISTIC OPERATIONS :—First among these we must mention the broad scattering of the gospel seed at the *Dendo Kwan*, opposite the main gate of the Osaka Exposition. This work is unique in the history of Japan missions, and has far exceeded the expectations of the most sanguine. Some estimate it as the greatest

---

* Miss Pratt.

piece of work in the way of direct evangelism ever undertaken in this land. It has been union work, and for four weeks the Nihon Kirisuto Kyōkwai workers took their turn. From eight to thirteen meetings were held daily, and an average of 1400 or 1500 have listened each day to the preaching. A large amount of literature was distributed, and many formed the determination to further investigate the matter after their return home. This has been the striking religious work of the year, and possibly reached as many people as the whole Taikyo Dendō movement, though that work could be followed up much better.

During the spring and early summer Japan was visited by Dr. Charles Cuthbert Hall and Dr. Pentecost; and many regrets were expressed that they were unable to extend the time of their stay.*

---

* Dr. Imbrie:—The visits of Drs. Hall and Pentecost were among the notable events of the year. Following is an account of their work in Tokyo.

The primary object of Dr. Hall in visiting Japan was to repeat, with certain changes, his course of lectures delivered in India on the Barrows Foundation. In Tokyo the course was given in the Hall of the Y. M. C. A. to good audiences made up chiefly but not exclusively of students; the majority of whom perhaps came from the Commercial College and Foreign Languages School. The lectures have since been published in English, and a translation into Japanese is soon to appear. In this way they will reach many who did not hear them. Besides delivering these lectures, Dr. Hall conducted the English service of the Union Church in the chapel of the Joshi Gakuin; and a translation of his sermon printed in the Fukuin Shimpo was highly appreciated by many. He also delivered a number of addresses: One at the reception given to him by the Tokyo pastors; others to the graduating classes of Meiji Gakuin and Aoyama Gakuin; and still another to the pastors and elders of the Church of Christ in Japan residing in Tokyo and the vicinity. These addresses may fairly be described as models. Dr. Hall seemed to know instinctively just what to say and said it admirably; and to a peculiar charm of speech there was added a peculiar charm of bearing. Most positive in his assertion of evangelical Christianity; deeply regretting the presence of the spirit of rationalism among some in Japan; he still, in the sense of the Apostle, made himself all things to all men.

The object of Dr. Pentecost in his visit was evangelistic in the more restricted meaning of the word. Careful preparation for his work was made by a joint-committee of the Tokyo Pastors Conference and the Evangelical Alliance in consultation with several missionaries. In the preliminary conference opinion was somewhat divided; some favoring especially meet-

The work of Dr. Franson in the north, especially in the Hokkaidō, is worthy of special remark.† Dr. Franson's work combined quietness and soberness and simplicity with a degree of power and kindling fire very seldom seen. He aimed to lead men to a conviction of their sins, and then to get them with their own lips to ask God's forgiveness; insisting on "Whosoever shall call upon the name of the Lord shall be saved." He believed that to ask men simply to study, or endeavor to enter the Christian life did not go far enough. He emphasized the gift of eternal life as a concomitant of the forgiveness of sins, and preached that as the foundation and starting point.

His meeting in the old Ainu chief's hut where for two hours he wrestled like Jacob with God in prayer over the old man, until at last the Ainu admitted that he had

---

ings in halls or theatres for the general public, and others rather meetings in half a dozen or more churches in different parts of the city with the special intention of strengthening evangelical belief and quickening the evangelistic spirit. On further consideration the latter view prevailed; but in order to let no opportunity slip unimproved it was agreed that four or five public meetings should be arranged for, as well as a number designed particularly for ministers Bible-women and such like. The arrangements included also the conduct by Dr. Pentecost of the English service in the Union Church in Tokyo on the three Sundays of his stay in the city; a visit to Maebashi, and two series of meetings in Yokohama, one for the Japanese and one for the foreign residents. When this plan had been tentatively accepted, one of the missionaries above referred to as in consultation with the joint-committee went to Kyoto to submit the plan to Dr. Pentecost and to receive any suggestions that his experience at home or in Japan might supply; and also to express to him the desire of the committee that he select as his themes at the meetings for the workers and also at those to be held in the churches, the distinctively evangelical doctrines of Christianity; a desire which the committee well knew would accord with his own wishes. With some slight changes in matters of detail the plan was accepted by Dr. Pentecost most cordially. Subsequently however it proved necessary to omit a number of the meetings arranged for, on account of his evident weariness; the result of the severe strain to which he had been put during the preceding six months, together with a certain something in the climate of Japan which affected him. On receiving word from Dr. Pentecost, the best halls available were secured; the churches selected (the pastor in each being invited to preside; notices of Dr. Pentecost's life and of the meetings to be held inserted in the news-

† Mrs. Pierson.

committed sin, and with his own lips prayed, "Lord Jesus, forgive my sins," is a scene that will never be forgotten, and which marks a distinct epoch in our Ainu work. Afterwards he got two other younger Ainu men to confess their sins and ask for forgiveness. To anyone knowing the stubborn self-righteousness of the Ainu men, and especially that of the proud dignified old chiefs, the transaction in that Ainu hut was nothing more nor less than a miracle of God. And so, indeed, had Dr. Franson prayed." Oh, Lord, if it takes a miracle to unlock this men's lips and to cause him to ask forgiveness, work the miracle, we beseech thee."

Another never to be forgotten meeting held by Dr. Franson was for the Christian workers of Asahigawa, men and women. In this he showed us that God not only tolerated but actually needed our help, (Judges 5 : 32);

---

papers; and circulars in large numbers printed and widely distributed through the churches.

The meetings intended especially for workers suffered no doubt from a difficulty hard to avoid. The Hall of the Y. M. C. A. was selected as on the whole the room most conveniently located; but Tokyo is a very large city, and a good attendance of workers meant a ride or a long walk on the part of many. It was much more convenient for most to attend the meetings in the churches. Accordingly when at the beginning of the second week, on account of Dr. Pentecost's condition, it was found necessary to reduce the number of his appointments, these meetings were among those selected for omission.

The meetings for the general public also were somewhat disappointing. Their wide advertizement in the newspapers and by other means failed to attract the audiences hoped for. So far as the student class was concerned, the time of the visit was the time for their examinations; and of the days set for these particular meetings one proved to be rainy. To these facts must be added the difficulties—the almost insurmountable difficulties—in the way of a speaker accustomed to address audiences which believe in the existence of one personal living God. When such a speaker attempts to put himself upon the plane and to adapt his materials to the understanding of a promiscuous audience in Japan, he attempts a task hard for him to appreciate and still harder to accomplish. For to many in his audience the thought of one personal living God is a new or nearly new conception, and to others a conception not new but in clear contradiction to all deep thinking; while, so far as worship is concerned, those who worship at all worship *Kamis* and *Hotokes*, ancestral ghosts and imaginary foxes.

This is a point regarding which a stranger in Japan preaching to the to the masses is almost sure to err. The audiences are attentive; but it is

that we can hasten Christ's coming by doing our work quickly(Jer. 48 : 10); that like the builders of the wall (Neh 5 : 3) we must work side by side in unity and harmony to save souls; that we must not only preach but " disciple " men (Matt 28 : 19); that we must " speak so " that " great multitudes " may " believe " (Acts 14 : 1); that we must have the worker's peace, the peace of those sent (John 20 : 21) ; that we must understand the command to " remit sins," i.e., to speak with souls until they feel that they are no longer bound by their sins, but are free; that we must do both the work of the pastor who plants and prepares the ground and sows, as well as that of the evangelist who waters, gathers in the crop and hands the new believer over for further tender care to the pastor.

Afterwards when questions were called for, it was

---

easy to mistake courtesy or curiosity for spiritual interest. At the close of an address an invitation may be given to such as are willing to accept Christ to rise. The invitation may be put in such a form as to express only an intelligent earnest reception of the gospel and many may rise; but those who really understand what they are professing are few and far between. Yet the speaker goes away with a very different impression. This was not the case with Dr. Pentecost; in fact he seldom called upon those who heard him for an immediate decision. On the other hand, Dr. Torrey in an account given in the Christian Herald of July 22nd, writes thus:—" After we got well started, there was rarely ever a meeting for the Japanese without a good many definite conversions. Japan had just been passing through a time of great religious awakening, and was thoroughly ready to hear the Gospel. In one city, where we spoke for two days, there were 119 who professed to accept Christ; and in another city, where we held five services in one day, 82 persons mostly men, in a single service, stood up to say that they would accept Jesus Christ as their personal Saviour, surrender to him as their Lord and Master, confess him as such publicly before the world, and strive to please him in everything. Some of the services were held in churches, others in halls and theatres, and many in schools and colleges. There were in all about 1,000 Japanese who professed to accept Christ. Among them some who declared that the meeting at which they were converted was the first Christian service they had ever attended, and that they never heard the Gospel before." Such statements may be verbally accurate; but they are misleading. We often speak of the old and simple story. In Christendom it is old and simple, but not in Japan; in Japan it is almost new, and to the multitudes it is strange. During the past year, the additions to the Church of Christ in Japan (Nihon Kirisuto Kyokwai), with all its pastors, evangelists, Bible-women, Christian schools and Council of Co-operating Missions, numbered in all 1075.

touching to see our pastors, some nearly as old as the apostolic man in our midst, eagerly and with the greatest confidence, and yet with humility and the deepest respect, put question after question to him:—How to care for young converts, What holiness means, How much of prayer ought to be communion, and how much petition, How can you know which of two ways is God's will. Truly he was a man sent to us from God; and he seemed to live his maxim of "constant, conscious communion with God."

Some lantern meetings have been held in villages, but not a great many. A lantern has its uses in collecting audiences, and in instruction; but its need is evidently not especially felt at present. Some missionaries have been able to extend their operations to villages. Some of the bodies of

---

The meetings in which Dr. Pentecost did his most successful work were those held in the churches, including among them the Chuo Kwaido; and of these there were ten in all. In every case the congregation was a good one; and in nearly every case the building was filled. It was generally understood that the meetings were intended especially for Christians; and those present were for the most part Christians, with perhaps in every case a number of those more or less interested in Christianity. The meeting in the Chuo Kwaido however was chiefly composed of students. Two of the most effective of the addresses were the one in the Chuo Kwaido on Christ the Light of the World, and the one in Shiba Church on Regeneration. Dr. Pentecost's method was to assert a number of points connected with his theme with emphasis and then to illustrate fully. Perhaps the impression made would have been clearer, if he had taken a somewhat smaller number of points and established them more perfectly by exposition and argument. It would also have been possible to reproduce the addresses in the Fukuin Shimpo more succinctly and effectively, if the didactic element had been proportionately greater; but many of the illustrations were telling and were listened to with marked attention. One of the pastors in the city summed up the general results as follows:—"The congregations were not greatly moved in feeling or to action; but many of those present were much interested." On the general question of the proper sphere for evangelistic work done by visitors the opinion expressed by a number of the best informed Japanese ministers was that results are to be looked for almost exclusively among Christians, or at least among those already well instructed in the truths of Christianity.

Besides his work among the Japanese, Dr. Pentecost conducted the English service in the Union Church on Sundays. The congregations were large; and many of those present spoke of the pleasure and profit with which they had heard him. He was kindly, sympathetic, earnest; and in spite of his weariness unshrinking in his work.

37

Christians too have undertaken operations of a similar nature, and with the doing of the work have become more enthusiastic. A great many village girls now come to the large cities to attend literary or industrial schools. Their stay may be for years, or only a few weeks. These girls are unusually susceptible to influence while thus in the town; and even after their return, not only remember what they learned from contact with Christians and missionaries, but welcome their friends at their own homes later. In this latter point they are likely to have their own way even though their parents are strong Buddhists. We all know the peculiar skill of the "Flower of the family" in having her own way, whether in Japan or the United States. One is inclined to think strongly that when we are once able to enter vigorously upon village work, we shall be surprised at the preparedness of the soil.

Work among soldiers has been successfully carried on at Asahigawa.* "This has been carried on regularly by a preaching service on Sunday afternoons at our clubhouse for soldiers, situated about half way between the town and the barracks. The hymn singing (of the Mitani Gospel Hymns) and the baby organ attract the soldiers who come and go in crowds, and listen fairly well to the short, simple sermons. The work is now supported by the Presbyterians only, but some of the other pastors kindly help with the preaching. A prayer-meeting immediately follows, and after this a Bible class is held for inquirers. All receive suitable soldier tracts and a copy of the *Toki-no-koe*.

An English Bible-class formerly held in the same place, especially for the soldiers or petty officers, now meets in our house twice a week, at which several sergeants and one or two lieutenants attend. Recently six of these have confessed their sins to God, and sought his aid to begin the Christian life. During the year five sergeants have received baptism and attend church regularly."

---

* Mrs. Pierson.

The Hiroshima "Corresponding Evangelism" scheme† is still kept up. It has become self-propagating, and numbers 411 at present. The "Gospel Message," emanating from the same place, has a larger circulation; and since Jan. 1st has grown in popularity on account of a Bible study department. Evangelists are requesting larger numbers for circulation instead of tracts. Twelve baptisms are reported as a direct result of this work, and there are still candidates besides. The *Yakō* is published fortnightly at Fukui,* the Bible lesson being the main feature. About a thousand copies are printed. The *Shin Seimei*, published by the pastor of the East Church of Osaka, is highly spoken of; and in Kyūshū it is proposed to distribute about 200 copies among the Christians, together with a Kyūshū supplement, giving information concerning the growth of the kingdom in the island. The idea is that in this manner all the benefits of a local newspaper can be secured, with a minimum of labor and expense. The Christians at Susaki, Shikoku, have shown a fine evangelistic spirit, selling 300 copies of the tract *Sankōryō* from door to door. For a time it was the talk of the town.

There are excellent reports in regard to Bible selling. Some never hold a meeting without selling a few copies of the Gospels and *Sankōryō* at its close. Near Matsuyama 100 Testaments were sold in one village.† In Yamaguchi Ken Bible selling has been prosecuted with astonishing results. Two Bible sellers are kept on the road all the time. Mr. McAlpine sells many Scriptures at meetings and on trains; the five *sen* Testament is an especially good seller. Miss Deyo has sold fifty Bibles, and Miss Winn matches it with fifty Testaments. Many speak of people coming to the house for Christian literature. Mr. Worley has success in selling Bibles on the street between the two temples of Ise. Mr. Loomis tells us that the problem of Bible work in Japan is not now as formerly, how we shall find a sale for our publications,

---

* Mr. G. W. Fulton.   † Mr. Bryan.

but how to keep a proper supply for the large and increasing demand. The demand for English Scriptures continues to be large.

The conclusion seems to be that we can do much more than we are doing in the line of circulation of the Scriptures; and as the religious knowledge and general knowledge of the nation increases, we may expect to see work done by the Spirit through the Word where other agencies have been quite wanting.

One of our number* is much impressed with the value of the *Fukuin Shimpō, Toki-no-Koe* and a number of other such newspapers. He has found them helpful to himself, and very useful for distribution. There is no doubt that every missionary would find his knowledge of the Japanese Church and his love for it and interest in it greatly increased by a regular reading of the *Fukuin Shimpō*. We cannot be too grateful that we have a Church paper so sound in doctrine, so evangelistic in spirit, and so thoroughly wide-awake and sensible. The Japanese evangelists find it most useful for themselves and their inquirers.

Kanazawa's experiment in Bible selling is of interest.†
"For the past two years the missionaries of the three Churches working here have subscribed five *yen* per month, and we have had a grant of a similar amount from the Bible Societies Committee. With these ten *yen* we have rented a little shop in a good place for a branch of the Fukuinsha of Osaka. They provide the stock and run the store. Our only connection with it is that we provide the place for them rent free, and in return are given a supervision of their stock to see that only suitable Christian literature is sold. As we are entering our third year with them, and the business is growing, we are proposing that they assume a part of the rent themselves as the first step toward entire independence. The results speak for themselves as follows.

---

* Mr. H. W. Myers † Mr. Dunlop.

	Scriptures sold	Other Christian books	
	Yen	Yen	Yen
1st year	149	225	374
2nd year	171	420	491

There are doubtless other cities where a similar plan might be made to work."

Work for fallen women has been engaged in by Miss Youngman, Mrs. McCauley and Mrs. Pierson. The first two have assisted in various ways the inter denominational Rescue Home. A new building to accommodate thirty-five women is nearing completion. It is pleasant to read, " This work has been a success thus far, and we hope may be a place where many may be led to know the true and living way." There are fourteen in the Home at present. From Mrs. Pierson's report we gather that at Asahigawa they now know how to apply the methods for rescuing girls from the brothels, and are doing so vigorously and fearlessly, with some failures it is true but still with considerable success. Three keepers of these houses in Asahigawa have recently given up the business for the reason explicitly given that Christianity was too much for them. This is all union work.

A report of the work of Miss Youngman fits in well under this head. It comprises the Kamejima Mission, the Ueno Mission, that at Kamakura and that at Koyama. She puts forth considerable effort for the Meguro Leper Home, which is proving a blessing to many. Industrial work has been begun at Fujioka Mura in Shizuoka Ken. Miss Youngman notes the great difference in the attitude of the people now compared with what it was when she landed in Yokohama thirty years ago. She deplores the results of the hasty baptisms of the Taikyo Dendo year, but rejoices in unbounded opportunities for teaching and influencing.

LITERARY WORK:—Under this head we would note that the translation of Lange's Japanese Grammar, soon to be published, is the work of one of our missionaries, Mr. Noss; and that Mr. Landis has put much time on the preparation of the map which is to be published shortly with funds left over after the expenses of the Tokyo Conference have been defrayed. Mr. McNair has worked, probably slaved, a good deal in connection with the new Union Hymn Book. His labors have been no easier on account of the impatience of the large body of people waiting for the day of publication, their old hymn-books gradually falling to pieces before their eyes. If extension of time can do anything toward making a good book, this will certainly be a good one. Our attention-has been called to the fact that there are to be two different editions with tunes. One is to be furnished with the ordinary staff notation, the other is the same with the addition of the air written in the tonic sol-fa notation just above the staff. The price of the two editions is to be the same. It would be a strange man who would not prefer the edition with the sol-fa notation additional. We should be very grateful that Mr. Allchin's persistence secured this.

CHURCH MUSIC :—Kyoto is the only place that indicates enthusiasm in the matter of church music. There the people meet and practice before service.* In the Church at large, some think little advance has been made; others† feel sure of great advance. More are laboring to improve the music than reported. Mr. Sakai, who has made a special study of music in America, has returned full of enthusiasm ; and has been visiting the churches with the improvement of music in mind. He has now started a school for the purpose in Tokyo. We wish him God-speed.

It is a fact that the number of those who can sing well and play the organ passably, is greatly increasing even in the smaller cities. The people are exerting themselves to get better organs. The mission schools have affected this greatly, and the great advance in the interest in music in the national schools has helped much. With the advent of the new hymn-book we may expect a decided

---

* Mr. Curtis.

advance in this respect. Perhaps nothing better could be suggested than that with the coming of the new hymn-book we should lay aside the old hymns that have been learned incorrectly and can never be unlearned, and take up an entirely new selection.

SABBATH OBSERVANCE:—Not a great deal is reported about this; but it seems that things are best in the Hokkaido, worst in Shinshū, and bad enough everywhere. However, out of the depths of the many disappointments in this respect, probably every missionary could give his instance of encouraging faithfulness on the part of individuals. Certainly of those who do observe the Sabbath carefully, more do so as a result of personal conviction than formerly. It might be profitable for us each to consider what changes have come in our own standard of Sabbath observance since landing in this country.

The following from the Hokkaido is encouraging. "The *Kyōfūkwai* of our city (Asahigawa) recently carried around to all the Christians of the town, a letter urging Sunday observance. The gist of it was that the great reason why the Church now-a-days is unspiritual and cold, is because it does not use God's appointed means of gaining spiritual life and power. Where God's appointed time is kept holy, there is life and progress. That we may sincerely serve God wholly, we urge that all Christians store-keepers close all day Sunday and hang out a Sunday closing sign; that all Christian employees ask for Sunday rest, and agitate for the closing of e.g. railroad shops, every Sunday; that all Christians now compelled to work on Sunday, seek employments that admit of Sunday rest, and that all making new engagements take such work only as admits of such rest; and that the day be spent in spiritual culture and evangelistic work."

"This letter was submitted first to the Temperance Society; and after 22 members present had endorsed it individually, the society as a whole adopted it and voted to have it carried from house to house among the Christians of our four Churches, Episcopal, Methodist, Congregational and Presbyterian, and signatures secured. A committee of six was appointed to do the work including the pastors' wives and a Bible-woman. After two earnest, indeed remarkable, prayer-meetings, the very arduous, difficult and delicate work was carried on during several weeks, resulting in 150 signatures received. Only one or two of our Christians declined to sign, and many candidates for baptism gladly signed. The improvement in the attendance at all the churches was marked, and a very deep spiritual impression was made. At its close the churches united in a praise meeting for the result. At this meeting the four yards and more of signatures were unfurled with devout thanks to God.

One of the most portentous things, and one against which we should use every influence, is the Sunday *shimbokkwai*, or social. A number of times of late reference to such meetings has appeared in the press. A new preacher arrives, and after the service a *kwangeikwai*; after an installation service, tea and cake are served. A *shimbokkwai* can be carried on in a spirit quite in keeping with the Sabbath, and there are occasions when the serving all of refreshments at a Sunday gathering may be right; but it is a move along the line of the least resistance, and one which can easily gain an acceleration that will fasten on us a custom that will be deadening to spiritual life."*

TEXT-BOOK SCANDAL:—Nothing has occurred for many years that has given the Japanese people such a moral shock as has the text-book scandal. Those entrusted with the instruction of the young have been so implicity relied upon, it was so positively believed that good morals were the necessary consequence of good education, that the revelation that the morals of many of those most prominent in the instruction of youth, men indeed of excellent education, were most corrupt, was bound to be shocking. The whole Japanese people are ashamed of the matter, and we who are only sojourners in the land feel that these men have wronged even us.

---

* Mrs. Pierson.

But the effect has been salutary. The preachers have made good use of it. The conclusions have not always been logically drawn, but the application has been so plain that few could miss it. This revelation has done more to convince the educated classes that the moral instruction in vogue is not meeting the requirements of the times than could years of preaching. The entirely changed attitude of the educational workers is doubtless due in no small degree to this event. In addition to this, many are coming to feel that moral instruction alone or a moral life alone, is not sufficient. We continually meet those who feel that they must have a religion of some kind or other.

SPIRITUAL LIFE :—Many encouraging things are said about the spiritual life of the churches and the character of the preaching. Doubtless there are many prayer-meetings poor enough, but from Matsuyama* we hear that there could not be better prayer-meetings than they have had. In Kagoshima, too, they have been specially good, numbering in attendance often more than half that of the Sunday service. Christian Endeavor methods are used in a number of places with good success.

Many will echo this sentiment of Dr. A. D. Hail: " The type of preaching of both pastors and evangelists is improving. It is becoming more scriptural and evangelical, more plain and practical. The power of the gospel is becoming to them more than a sounding phrase, and more than mere cant."

There is nothing exceptional about the following testimony :† " It seems to me that it can safely be said that the thermometer of the Church does indicate a warmer spiritual life. There are more non-professional individuals working for individuals ; women especially, who have been Christians for years without feeling any personal responsibility in the salvation of others, are now manifesting a disposition to try and do something for their friends. Recent converts too seem to come into the new life with

---
* Mr. Bryan.   † Mrs. MacNair.

a fuller sense of its meaning and their own personal blessing, and the need of bringing their countrymen and women to the same light and life." The missionaries at large are reading the same signs.

Meetings of the evangelists have been reported from two points. The action of Daikwai (Synod) allowing evangelists to become corresponding members of Chukwai (Presbyteries) has had a good effect; and in Kyūshū advantage was taken of this to have all the workers meet for two days after the Chūkwai. The results were most happy. All distinction of Japanese and foreign was lost sight of, and most wholesome and helpful conference indulged in. As to the relations between the pastors and evangelists and the missionaries, a Tokyo missionary* expresses the state of the case for the whole country when he says, "The relations between our missionaries and the leading spirits among the Japanese brethren seems to me to be as cordial as one could expect or wish."

But the best word in regard to evangelists' meetings comes from Hiroshima.† We gave it in full. "Efforts have been made during the year to infuse the evangelists with a more earnest desire for souls, and with a desire for a deeper spiritual life. By prayer with the men on the various trips, by a meeting in connection with the spring meeting of Presbytery, and by a workers' meeting at my home in the fall, we have endeavored to feed and build up the faith and zeal of the men. It is gratifying to note that the men themselves feel the need of a deeper spiritual life. In both fields of the Sanyo Presbytery, we have sent all the evangelists to this workers' meeting in connection with the spring meeting. Questions of practice and policy have been left entirely out, and practical and applicable Biblical subjects have been considered. The effect has been quite noticeable. Also, profiting by the results reported by some members of the last Council, although with fear and trembling because of a former experience, the evangelists were invited to a workers'

---

* Dr. Haworth. † Mr. Brokaw.

meeting here in town in the fall. Some of the subjects were, The Prayer Life of the Evangelist, The Intellectual Life of the Evangelist, The most Common Error in Preaching. A preaching service with communion afterwards was helpful to all, and the men went back to their fields with a new determination and a new purpose. During the year also, we have made it a practice to call one or two evangelists to one of the outstations, and with them hold a two days special preaching service. That enabled them to meet with each other, to engage in work of mutual helpfulness; and enabled the missionary, always being present also, to informally urge on to the greatest zeal. A prayer circle was formed at the fall workers' meeting, each station being prayed for in turn, and all uniting on Sunday to pray for the salvation of Japan.

One of the results of these various forms of work for the evangelists themselves, besides the result of deepening the spiritual life and quickening zeal, has been the working out of a mutual sympathy between the evangelists themselves, and the evangelists collectively and individually and the missionary. So far as I am aware, all jealousies have been sunk out of sight, and between us all a new love and fellowship has worked out. Townsend says in his Asia and Europe, that there is a veil in the life of each Asiatic beyond which no European ever goes; and that the inner secrets are guarded even against most intimate friends. However that may be, I am convinced now that we can all get really close to these men; and thus not only win their confidence, but secure their best effort."

THE DENDO KYOKU:—Brief reference has been made above to the work of the Dendo Kyoku (Board of Home Missions). In many respects it is quite like another mission likewise co operating with the Nihon Kirisuto Kyokwai (Church of Christ in Japan). Since a large part of its funds comes from churches and preaching places still receiving aid from the missions, it might be feared that its activity would work disadvantageously. Fortunately, this does not seem to be true. One the contrary it seems to have a stimulating effect, and to improve the financial tone. Dr. Haworth visited its work in Formosa this spring, and we introduce with approval the following from him : " I feel that we ought to foster the interest of the Church in its own Board of Missions in every way we can. Its work in the past, though probably worthy of criticism in matters of detail, really seems to me to warrant the utmost confidence. What I saw of its work in Formosa, where it has operated absolutely apart from missionary relations, sufficiently proves to me its ability to do the work it is undertaking. Its entering into China during the present year seems to me full of significance ; the very small beginning of the day we all hope and pray for, when the Japanese missionary will become a prominent factor in the regeneration of that empire. And in working out the destiny of the Nihon Kirisuto Kyokwai ultimately to cover every part of the empire, the Dendo Kyoku must be a very important factor."

We learn from the secular papers that Japanese teachers and advisers are being extensively introduced into China. However startling the idea may strike us at first, we must heartily rejoice that the Japanese Church, through its Board of Missions is preparing to send religious teachers to that empire. In the spring Mr. Segawa and Mr. Kiyama visited North China at the request of Japanese Christians there. Since their return Mr. Maruyama has been despatched to Tien Tsin to work for the Chinese ; and we now learn that Mr. Sagawa, who has so long been the Nestor of the Kyūshū forces, is soon to sail for Tien Tsin to look after the work among the Japanese. It would seem that such men cannot well be spared from this country at such a time as this, but yet we know that there is that scattereth and yet increaseth. In some cases growth is best promoted by a division that seems to promise only weakness.

NEEDS :—Expression has been made of a number of needs. For instance, mission families are needed at Toyama, at Moji and at Oita. The (German) Reformed Mission feels that it is needed in the Hokkaido, and Dr. Haworth thinks that one of our missionaries ought to be located in Formosa. Mr. Price suggests that small libraries of Christian books be put in government schools. He also voices the need of proper theological works translated into Japanese. Mr. Fulton thinks that Trumbull's Individual Work for Individuals might be translated with profit. Mr. Jones of wishes for a book containing a simple and brief statement what it means to be a Christian. Mrs. McCauley desires a set of lessons on the life of Christ for primary classes.

SUGGESTIONS:—This is not just the heading I wish but it sounds better than New Themes, which is what first suggested itself.

At Takamatsu* they have been troubled because candidates for baptism, while very faithful during the period of instruction, show a tendency, after receiving the sacrament, to become remiss, some quite falling back. They have adopted the practice of not baptizing till at least three months after a satisfactory examination has been passed. Mr. Pieters also has raised the question whether it might not be well for the missionary invariably to baptize only after a second examination. During the interval the candidate's earnestness of purpose might be more fully tested. This is certainly not what Presbyterians are used to, but may not our present conditions call for some such uniform practice?

A number have expressed a desire that more care be taken to introduce members making a change of residence to new church relationships, even in other bodies of Christians, where necessary.

At Tokushima,† in addition to distributing Christian newspapers, a point is made of lending religious books; special pains being taken that they do not vanish like the dew.

Mr. Price urges more coöperation with one another, more pride in our own Church and a more fixed purpose to

---

* Mr. W. C. Buchanan.   † Mr. H. W. Myers.

extend the peculiar excellencies of our sober and orthodox Church over the land. He thinks coöperation can be carried to an extreme, and deplores coöperation with those who are not sound in the faith.

Viscount Watanabe recently expressed himself favorably to Christianity. His words were re-printed and many hundred copies distributed in the neighborhood of his native place. The use of the daily papers as a medium for reaching the people has been suggested for those able to do it.* At Kagoshima the daily paper prints gratis each week announcements of the Sunday services with subjects of discourses.

From one of the girls-schools in the North† comes the word, " Our best work is done in the Home, where we come in daily contact with eight girls." The Japanese Government has gone in heavily for female education. A few years ago our schools stood out prominently. This prominence is fast going. The girls pursuing studies above Koto Sho Gakko grade in every large city are numbered by hundreds. Some cities have far above a thousand. Except the few in the dormitories, these girls board here there and all over. Would it not be possible for single-lady missionaries to gather ten or a dozen or even twice that number of girls into a nearly self-supporting Home under their supervision; and thus exert a good deal of that influence which heretofore it has been possible to exert only when the expensive machinery of a girls-school was maintained. Until the experiment is tried, we can know little of what can be done; but at first sight this would seem like an broad field of opportunity.

With this we close our review of the evangelistic part work.

During the year it has seemed good to the Lord of the Harvest to remove from active labors Dr. T. T. Alexander and Mr. A. M. Drennan, each of twenty years and upwards of service. Our only word will be, How thoroughly they would have enjoyed adding their labors to ours in these times of great opportunity.

* Mr. H. K. Miller.   † Miss Rose.

With the exception of schools for theological training, the educational institutions conducted by the missions of Council report themselves as enjoying a prosperity far in advance of that heretofore known. Most of them are literally overflowing.

There are eleven boarding schools for girls carried on. We are stronger in this respect than in most others. It may be a question whether it would not be better to have one or two less girls-schools and one or two boys-schools in their stead; or a question whether these schools are distributed over the country to the best advantage. But the facts are that we have the schools; the capital invested is drawing interest as never before; and the one thing apparently to do now is to work them for all they are worth. No one reading the reports in full can fail to be impressed with the strong Christian character of these schools, and the evangelistic work going on within them and proceeding from them as a centres.

Schools for boys are in better condition than ever before. There are still many disadvantageous things in connection with their conduct, but such as the schools are a full quota of students can be secured, and teachers of better literary and religious qualifications than formerly are to be had. Private schools are receiving greater consideration at the hands of the Government. Meiji Gakuin and Tohoku Gakuin are recognized by the Department of Education as of Chū Gakko grade; their graduates can pass without examination into Semmon Gakko, and it is hoped that shortly the same will be true in regard to Koto Gakko. But best of all, our schools are different from other schools not so much as being foreign as being Christian.

It is hard to believe that we have the schools of Chū Gakko grade that we ought to have. If the Hokkaido needs a girls-school, it certainly needs a Christian boys-school. We are thankful for a Christian Academy in Kyūshū, at Nagasaki; but it seems all wrong that our

Council is not represented by a boys-school in the long stretch from Tokyo to Shimonoseki.

Similarly, it is a matter for rejoicing that we have two good schools for the training of evangelists, one at Tokyo and one at Sendai; but we must ever bear in mind that some day we must have another such school somewhere between Tokyo and Kagoshima. It is true that we have not the funds for it at present, and it needs to be erected at some point where there is a stronger body of believers than we have at any point except Osaka just now. The times evidently are not ripe for this yet, but a theological school with a literary Koto-kwa below it, and possibly a Chū Gakko below that, will certainly be required for our Church before many years are past. The responsibility for this matter would seen to rest with the West Japan Presbyterian, the Southern Presbyterian, and the Cumberland Presbyterian Missions. But for the present, in regard to our boys-schools too, let us work our existing plants to full capacity, making sure of the quality of our work, while not forgetting the expansion called for by the future.

The number of ministers that, from all parts of the country, within a year or two, have resigned their charges and gone to the United States for study, is quite startling. It would seem that the Meiji Gakuin is in a position to facilitate this movement. There is always a keen sense of loss when a good man steps out of the work if only temporarily. But some men have come back from the United States with increased intellectual power, and having drunk deeply of the best spiritual inspiration the home-land affords. The movement is a natural one, perhaps inevitable. The missionary may not sweepingly approve, nor yet can he sweepingly condemn it. Since the condition exists, let us rather strive to gain the most possible good from it.

A Theological Schools.

(1) " The work in the Theological Department of the Meiji Gakuin has gone on much as usual. Two students pursuing the Higher Course in the Academic Department

are taking the course in Gospel History; and two others have expressed their intention of entering the ministry. Three Special Students have been admitted and two older men are in attendance. During the year Mr. Kashiwai, who has been teaching Church History for a number of of years, has been ordained to the ministry and installed as a professor. Since then he has gone to America and expects to spend the year at Princeton Theological Seminary; the Seminary giving him a scholarship yielding $150 (gold). In connection with this it may be said that Dr. Ibuka has received a letter from Messrs. Baba and Kawazoi, saying that they had been most cordially welcomed by the faculty and students of Auburn Seminary, and that classes in English and Greek had been established for their special benefit. During the absence of Mr. Kashiwai a part of his work will be done by Mr. Hata, who has recently graduated at Princeton Semiary, and who divides his time between the Theological School and the Dai Machi Church. In conclusion it need hardly be said that the coming of Dr. Oltmans during the spring of next year is looked forward to with much pleasure."* Mr. Fulton adds, "I think we have some men of a good deal of promise in the student body to-day; men who seem to be in earnest, and whose careers will be watched with interest."

(2) The Theological Department of Tosan Gaku-in, Nagasaki, has been indefinitely suspended

(3) The Theological Department of the Tohoku Gaku-in, Sendai, is well equipped to do good work. It has two courses of study; the one intended for men with a knowledge of English and a good preparation, and the other for those whose preparation has not been so complete. There were no graduates last year, but there are nine men receiving instruction.

B Bible Training Schools.

(1) For women. Seisho Gakkwan, Tokyo. East Japan Presbyterian Mission.

---

* Dr. Imbrie.

This school reports no graduates this year. Family reasons, sickness and the demand for brides in Hawaii broke up the class. The brides are reported as doing good work in Hawaii; but we agree with the sentiment expressed, that they could have done better work if they had waited to complete the course.

* " Seventeen were left in the school, four of these being wives of theological students. There have been years when we have had greater numbers; but I do not recall a time when we had students more faithful, or more appreciative of their opportunities for study. One of the features of this year's work has been the special attention paid to the preparation of the Sunday-school lessons. The results have been most satisfactory, as shown in the development of the individual woman, and in more successful teaching. During the winter, the students have carried on five Sunday-schools in Tokyo and Shinagawa. The upper class has spent two afternoons each week visiting in the homes of the Sunday-school children. Fortunately two of the experienced graduates, having a few months between engagements, are helping to keep up the work in all these schools while the older students, either with Bible-women or alone, are working in the country for three or six months. Last year's summer work in two country districts was of so much interest and had such good results, that Bible women were sent in response to urgent requests to continue the work through the year. The work goes on with increased interest and there have been a number of baptisms, eighteen as a result in one place."

Womans Union Mission, Yokohama.

In this school we find twenty or more in training, besides a good number engaged in actual work. While the women are in training, they have special house to house work in Yokohama, besides Sunday-schools and women's meetings." Increased interest in evangelistic work is reported.

---

* Mrs. MacNair.

(2) For men.

Dr. Murray is carrying on a Bible Training Class at Yamaguchi. He has three young men with him at present. His purpose is to give them instruction in the Bible and actual training in religious work that will make them more useful on returning to their home churches, or fit them to become evangelists or preachers if they desire to continue. The pupils have two hours of recitations each morning, and three times a week hold preaching services.

C Boys Boarding Schools.

Meiji Gakuin, Tokyo. Academic Department.

§ "The past year, while not characterized by any marked changes, has been a prosperous one. There was no change in the privileges granted us by the Government till after the close of the school year; but in May (1903) our pupils were put upon the same footing as those of government schools, so far as relates to entrance into special schools (Semmon Gakko, i.e. certain prefessional schools). We are still handicapped as regards entrance to the government High Schools (Koto Gakko). On account of the lack of this privilege quite a number of our pupil especially from the 4th year class, left at the end of the school year, so that they might enter government schools and by graduating from them, escape the handicap. If the new privilege had been granted a few weeks earlier, several of these might have remained, Still, in spite of these losses and very thorough pruning on our part, our number has increased a little and we now have 178 in actual attendance. The work has been much as in former years, and has been quite satisfactory to ourselves. The higher course now has pupils in all three of its classes, and they are all kept busy; but partly on account of lack of teachers and the consequent necessity of combining classes, the course has not yet been thoroughly systematized. We have not yet received for this department certain privileges that we expected.

---
§ Dr. Wyckoff.

The religious condition of the school has been good. The students Y. M. C. A. prayer-meeting has been well attended, and the meetings have been interesting and helpful. A number of the pupils have been holding an early morning prayer-meeting for several weeks past. There have been some changes in the Japanese teaching force, with the result that we now have a larger number of Christian Japanese teachers than we have ever had before. The new chapel is now in process of erection. Mr. J. C. Ballagh has recently returned from America, and is now teaching some classes; thus relieving Messrs. Landis and Wyckoff, who had more classes than they could properly attend to."

Statistics. Foreign teachers (including Mr. Ballagh) 3, Japanese teachers 14, Pupils 178, graduates 21, converts 9, Christians 44.

Tohoku Gakuin, Sendai. Academic Department.

* " This is the only Christian school for young men in the north-east of Japan. It now has an enrollment of 179 young men, 170 of these being in the Academic and 9 in the Theological Department. There were 8 graduates from the lower, or Chū Gakko Course, 4 from the Higher Course. Of these graduates 9 were baptized Christians. The number of baptisms in the school during the year was 11. The attendance of the students at morning prayers, at church services, Bible-classes and prayer-meetings was very good during the year. The Bible is taught regularly as one of the required branches. The working of the school has gone on regularly and steadily during the year. A high grade of scholarship has been aimed at, while at the same time such emphasis has been placed on spiritual development that while less than one-third of the students are baptized Christians, the whole school is pervaded by a Christian atmosphere to such an extent that the thoughts and ideas of the students are constantly being moulded by this influence, and many are ripening for an open profession of their

---

* Dr. Schneder.

faith. The teachers have worked faithfully, and unitedly, and have at the same time in the majority of cases been actively interested in direct Christian work, many of them being ready to go out into the country to do evangelistic work whenever called upon. The school has the military conscription postponement privilege for its Chū Gakko course."

Tosan Gakuin, Nagasaki.

*" The past year has been one of somewhat unusual experience for Steele College. In the first place, after a long period of uncertainty, it was decided by the Board that theological instruction be not given under present circumstances and conditions. A little later the family of Dr. Steele, the founder of the institution, furnished the means for making such provision, as will enable it to secure government recognition as a Chū Gakko. This, however, was so recent, that no steps have yet been taken to accomplish the object aimed at. The past has been a year of unusual perplexity in securing and retaining competent teachers, owing chiefly to the lack of appropriations to pay salaries to satisfy such men. However, there has been such a demand for education that as many students as could be accommodated in the lower classes have been entered and for the most part they continue in attendance. The difficulty lies in retaining them in the advanced classes. Should government recognition be secured and the equipment of the institution be improved, this defect would no doubt be remedied. Even as it is, the school has made a good record for the year in morals and religion.

Of the average of about a hundred students in attendannce, there has been no case requiring stringent discipline. The school Y. M. C. A. has about one half the students enrolled as active or associate members, of whom 19 are Christians. Thirteen have been received into the Church during the year. The interest in the truth continues, and there are candidates for baptism.

---

* Dr. Stout.

The class of five graduated in March are all Christians, one of them having gone to the Meiji Gaku-in to pursue the theological course. There is one young man in the present graduating class who is looking forward to the ministry."

D   Girls Boarding Schools.

Ferris Seminary, Yokohama.   Reformed Church in America.

* " This school was established in Yokohama in 1875, by the Board of Foreign Missions of the Reformed Church in America. There are at present four courses of study. 1. The Preparatory Course of three years. The studies of this course are chiefly the Japanese language, reading and writing, geography, arithmetic and one exercise a day in colloquial English. 2. The Grammar Course, which is four years, consists of a drill in the Japanese and English languages, universal geography, history, arithmetic, elementary physics, natural history, botany, physiology, hygiene and free-hand drawing. Pupils who enter this course from government schools are required to study English only for one year. 3. The English Normal course of three years was introduced in April of this year. The studies of the course consist of the English language and literature only. Graduates from Koto Jo Gakko may enter, and it is designed to meet the demand in some measure for teachers of English in the Sho Gakko. The pupils are given daily instruction in the Bible in all these courses. Daily systematic physical exercise is insisted upon. Instruction in sewing is given to all the school twice a week, also flower arrangement, *chanoyu* and etiquette to those who desire these accomplishments. Instruction in vocal music by the sol-fa method has produced excellent results. Instruction on the organ is supplied those who have the Bible course in view, and to others who pay the extra fees, also piano lessons are given to those who

---
* Mr. Booth.

desire and pay for them. 4. The Bible course consists of sacred history, introduction to the books of the Old and New Testament, sacred geography, biographical studies of the chief characters in the Old and New Testament, the coming Messiah in types, predictions, and in the advent. God's revelation of himself to man, or God seeking to make himself known to man and man's relation to God in worship, with practical studies in God's methods in training workers.

We have not yet seen our way clear to re open the higher course, chiefly through lack of funds. Recognition of its utility on the part of the mission and resolutions regarding the advisability of restoring this course to the institution fail to make it materialize. Serious difficulty has been experienced to obtain suitable Japanese teachers. Such a difficulty would be greatly minimized were we able as formerly to train the large part of our teachers by means of the higher course."

Statistics. Whole number of graduates from the Bible course, 3; number of graduates this year from the Grammar Course, 7; pupils enrolled, 115; members of the Church, 69; united with the church, 16; candidates for baptism, 4; number of pupils in attendance, 90; foreign teachers, 5; Japanese teachers, 6. Pupils are distributed as follows:—Bible course, 4; English Normal Course, 6; Grammar Course, 62; Preparatory, 18; Total, 90.

Woman's Union Mission, 212 Yokohama. Literary Department.

The school seems to have had a prosperous year, especially in spiritual things. It profited by a visit from Miss Doremus, the Secretary of the Board. It has seventy six pupils. A class of eight graduated; four of whom have remained as teachers. Special attention is given to physical exercise. Many desire to take organ lessons that they may be able to be helpful at religious meetings when going out to their homes. The school has been fortunate in securing the services of an unusually well qualified business manager.

Statistics. Pupils, 76; graduates, 8; foreign teachers, 2.

Joshi Gakuin, Tokyo. East Japan Presbyterian Mission.

* "The new school year which began in April opened with very bright prospects. Forty new pupils were admitted, and many more could not be received because there was neither dormitory nor class room accommodation for them.

Miss Ballagh and Miss Gardner are still in America; but during the year, the force of teachers has been strengthened, by the arrival of Miss Alexander. In March seven of the girls graduated, all of whom are now engaged in Christian work; one of them has gone to Honolulu to join her parents in work among the Japanese residing there. A number of the girls teach in churches and Sunday-schools in different parts of the city. The year has been one of quiet, steady work on the part of most of the pupils. It is a pleasure to report that just now at the close of another term eight of the girls are to be admitted to church membership.

Statistics. Boarding pupils, 110; day pupils, 109; total, 219. Graduates, 8; admitted to the Church, 9.

Naniwa Jogakko, Osaka. West Japan Presbyterian Mission.

The whole course of study extends over five years; the lowest year corresponding to the Koto Sho Gakko grade. There is in the school a large C. E. Society carried on successfully by the students and Japanese teachers; twelve teachers and students are engaged in Sunday-school work. A large Sunday-school with an average attendance of 90, and conducted by the Christian teachers and students, is held in the school chapel.

Statistics. Pupils, 45; Christians, 12; graduates, 12; united with the Church during year, 2; foreign teachers, 2; Japanese teachers, 8.

Hokuriku Jogakko, Kanazawa. West Japan Presbyterian Mission.

---

* Miss Helena Wyckoff.

* "The Hokuriku Jo Gakko, after a successful year of work, has begun a new year with a larger attendance than ever before in its history. Eight pupils have been enrolled since April first. Several have been laid aside because of illness, but there has been a daily attendance of seventy-five. The school has grown in favor very rapidly during the past two years; this year the number of pupils has just doubled. In the past, the school was largely attended by girls from the surrounding towns, while but few city girls applied for entrance; now the tide has changed, and our attendance is almost entirely from city homes. While this does not greatly increase the number of boarding pupils, it gives an entrance into the homes heretofore closed to us, and many opportunities for evangelistic work. Another encouraging outlook is the apparent interest the new pupils show in the religious life of the school; many of them becoming members of the Christian Endeavor and Temperance Societies. A fair number attend the church services quite regularly, while a number come frequently to the weekly church prayer-meetings; a rather unusual thing for day pupils to do. As the larger number of students in the school are new, the number of Christians is small. Several of last year's students have as yet failed to receive their parents' consent to be baptized. We hope these barriers will soon be swept away, and that before the term closes at least five of them may enter the Church. Of the three graduates in March, one has entered the kindergarten and one the Joshi Gakuin; while the third though as yet undecided, hopes to enter the latter school before long. All there were active Christians. The corps of Japanese teachers is more than usually efficient. Five are earnest Christians, doing active work both in the school and the churches. As the school has grown in numbers there has sprung up a fresh enthusiasm on the part of the students, which has lent a new impetus to study as well as to the social life of

---

* Miss Luther.

the school. Among the foreign teachers there have been a number of changes during the year. Miss Shaw, after thirteen years of service, was compelled to return to America because of ill health; and owing to lack of force and illness several changes have taken place which greatly disturbed the even tenor of the teaching, as well as the life in the home. But now things seem brighter; and as the outlook is so bright, the one aim for the future, is an increased efficiency in all departments."

Statistics. Pupils, 80; graduates, 3; foreign teachers, 3.

Kojo Jo Gakkō, Yamaguchi. West Japan Presbyterian Mission.

* " So far as success can be estimated by numbers this has been the most successful year in the history of the school; as the number enrolled has passed the limit fixed by the Educational Committee of the Mission in regard to this school, and the actual attendance now is at the very verge of becoming unlawful, according to the rules of the government as to the number of pupils per *tatami* (mat). The course of study provides for three years preparatory; but on account of limited space it was thought best at present to refuse all applicants for the first of these years. Three girls have united with the Church during the year. All the girls are members of the King's Daughters Society, and give one hour a week for work besides attending the weekly prayer-meeting. The school provides eight teachers in the Sunday-schools connected with our work. There is but one regular foreign teacher, but Miss Foster also gives several hours each week to the school."

Statistics. Pupils enrolled, 56; in regular attendance, 40; foreign teachers, 1; Japanese teachers, giving full time, 5; giving part time, 3.

Kinjo Jo Gakko, Nagoya. Southern Presbyterian.

† " At the Kinjo Jo Gakko the year has been one of quiet prosperity. After a two years struggle we have succeeded in securing a competent corps of Japanese teachers. The Christian girls have taught in two Sunday-

---

* Miss Palmer. † Miss Houston.

schools and have been most helpful in all the Christian meetings held in the school. Just as soon as a girl becomes a Christian she is expected to take her turn conducting the prayer-meetings. Eleven of the younger girls have recited the Child's Catechism, and received certificates. I hope they may soon complete the Shorter Catechism. Train up a child in the way it should go."

Statistics. Pupils, 68 ; Christians, 33 ; converts during the year, 15 ; graduates, 8 ; foreign teachers, 1 ; Japanese teachers, 8.

Wilmina Jo Gakko, Osaka. Cumberland Presbyterian Mission.

* "The attendance at our school has steadily increased during the last year, and now at the middle of the first term of the present school year, our actual attendance is 94, almost equal to the entire enrollment for the previous year. Of the 94, twenty are enrolled in the Primary grades, two years covering the usual Higher Primary grades of the public schools. Forty-nine pupils are in the four year Grammar Course, and six of these will graduate in June. The other 25 girls come for special studies, sewing, English or music. We permit pupils to take only part of the regular course if they desire ; and a number of girls too weak to undertake the full course are glad to enter for certain classes. I should be glad to know if any other school permits this. Our Japanese teachers seem to think not. They say the public schools do not ; and many weak children are therefore obliged to drop out of school. We have tried this plan for several years, and I have seen no serious objection to it while it certainly does give a valuable opportunity for study to girls who would otherwise go no higher than the lower Primary. Several who come for sewing principally take up two or three of the regular studies, especially reading and writing. We have all except a few of the music and English pupils in the Bible classes ; and the receptivity and response of all to religious thoughts and

---

* Miss Morgan.

spiritual application, has been a great pleasure; indeed almost a surprise, to the teachers. While most of the pupils are day pupils, and from non-christian homes, still we feel that the school is undoubtedly a great evangelizing agency in its general influence as well as its direct religious teaching. The homes of the pupils are open to our visits, and this year I have tried to make some use of this most valuable opportunity.

In last year's Council Report, there was a suggestion that a girls high-school be started in Osaka as the central point of the educational work done by our Coöperating Missions in West Japan. Personally I think the suggestion worth serious consideration, and the time not too premature for success. Of course the school should be a thoroughly equipped one in every respect; and, I think, centrally located in order to draw pupils from all quarters of this densely populated, compactly built, city. When the Joshi Gakuin reports all departments full and applications refused, it seems time we were opening such a school nearer home for our girls of the west who wish such advantages. I should be glad to see the suggestion taken up and pushed until such a school is opened either by one mission or the united missions."

Statistics. Enrolled, 97; average attendance, 60; foreign teachers, 3; Japanese teachers, 5.

Sturges Seminary, Nagasaki. Reformed Church in America.

* " The cholera epidemic of last summer delayed the opening of the fall term until October first. Our school year closed in March, when two girls were graduated from our higher course, and seven from the lower. From the beginning of the new year, the course became one of five years. The enrollment of last fall term was only fifty, but we had an unusally large entering class in April, raising the number to seventy-five. Of these, thirty-one are boarders and ten are Christians. Five girls have been baptized during the year, and nine others

---

* Miss Zurfluh.

are attending a voluntary class for enquirers. Our C. E. Society continues to be helpful. Besides the fourteen resident active members, we have five associate and fifteen corresponding members ; the latter composed of graduates. Some of the older girls help in the two Sunday-schools for children, which are conducted by teachers of the school. The King's Daughters meet once a week for sewing, knitting, etc. From their earnings they have contributed several small amounts to benevolent objects."

Statistics. Pupils, 75 ; graduates, 2 ; Christians, 10 ; converts, 5 ; foreign teachers, 2.

Miyagi Jo Gakko, Sendai. Reformed Church in the U.S.
* " On account of the burning of our school over a year ago, and for want of proper buildings, etc., we have been hampered in our work during the year past. We had 103 pupils enrolled, and the average monthly enrollment was 97. Thirty-two of these were Christians, six of whom were baptized during the year. We had about 44 boarders ; but if we had the room, we should have had double that number. We were obliged to refuse 40 pupils during the year because of want of room. We hope to be able to go into our new dormitory by September of this year. Our new recitation hall, the Christian Faust Memorial Building, has been begun ; but we shall not be able to occupy it for about a year. We shall however be able to carry on our work in the new dormitory for the time being. We had three graduates this year, two of whom are now doing Bible work, and one of whom has entered the Joshi Dai Gakko in Tokyo. Twelve of our own graduates have been employed as regular Bible-women during the year, and eight have done part teaching and part Bible work. By means of the Bible-women and teachers, and Christian pupils of the Girls School about twenty Sunday-schools in Sendai and vicinity have been supplied with teachers ; two or three girls, and sometimes more, going to one Sunday-school. Most of them taught in two Sunday-schools, and

---

* Zurfluh.

some also attended and took part at the evening services. God has blessed his work here richly; may he be glorified. It is interesting to note that the eight students who made up the highest class of the Government Koto Jo Gakko when it was opened, a year or so ago, were all graduates of mission schools. Two at least of these came from schools connected with the Council."

Statistics. Pupils enrolled, 103; Christians, 32; baptized during the year, 6; boarders, 44.

Hokusei Jo Gakko, Sapporo. East Japan Presbyterian Mission.

* "Our school opened the new year in April very encouragingly, and though we have not attained to the number one hundred and forty reported for last year, we seem in a fair way to do so, numbering one hundred and fifteen at the beginning of the new term. The interest in Christianity which pervaded the school last year, bringing twenty-three of our older pupils into the Church, seems to continue; and ten more received baptism just before we closed for the summer vacation. The new buildings which we have so much needed and have been praying and laboring for so long, are now not quite completed, but very nearly so, giving us hope that we may be able to occupy them in September as promised. Through the earnest labors of Mr. Landis in planning, and Mr. J. C. Ballagh in superintending the building, we have good comfortable buildings, accommodating sixty or seventy boarders, and a chapel that will seat as many as are likely to come. The Hokusei is a Koto Jo Gakko, a little higher in grade than the usual Government Koto Jo Gakko. The aim of the school is, like other mission schools, to give as good a secular education, with Christianity as a foundation, as possible in a limited number of years; the Bible being a daily text book."

Statistics. Pupils, 115; baptisms during the year, 23.

Seishu Jo Gakko, Otaru. East Japan Presbyterian Mission.

---

* Miss Smith.

* " At the Otaru school the year has been one of quiet growth. It is blessed with two of the best of Japanese teachers, graduates of the Joshi Gakuin. They are an inspiration. Then too the pastor of our Otaru Presbyterian Church lends his efficient services to the senior class three afternoons a week. There is a good degree of interest in the daily Bible classes, and English and music are very popular. There is unusual enthusiasm in the Kindergarten Department this spring. Our small quarters are overflowing. I was much interested to read in the Council Report of last year that the investigation committee for girls-schools found the verdict, ' Never before did school work for girls appear so valuable or so desirable; and the fact is our school work is evangelistic work, and valuable evangelistic work at that.' Let us thank God and take courage."

Statistics. Pupils, 50; Kindergarten Department, 75; graduates, 3; Christians, 5; united with the Church during the year, 2; foreign teacher, 1; Japanese teachers, 5.

It will be observed that there is great irregularity in the statistics presented. More reliable statistics will be found in the report of the Statistical Committee. The above are little more, in some cases, than a culling of facts given in the body of the report. However, since some facts are referred to that do not find their way in the regular statistical tables, it has been thought best to let them stand.

DAY SCHOOLS

The report under this head is not so complete as we should like; but since it was possible for us only to use the materials that came to hand, we could hardly do better.

Kanazawa Kindergarten.

Sixteen children graduated from this kindergarten in March. There are now forty-five enrolled, and a number on the waiting list. The daily attendance is kept at about

---

* Miss Rose.

this figure, for a child who is absent for a month has his place filled by the child who stands first on the waiting list. The closing of the primary school has given much needed room. The yard space also is much enlarged, and the vegetable garden allowed the janitor is made to do service as a source of instruction. There is a desire to have more pupils. This involves more teachers ; and as a matter of economy, in the broad sense, kindergarteners are being trained in connection with the work. This is giving satisfaction, the normal pupils having entered lovingly and happily into the spirit of the kindergarten. These assistants join with the head kindergartener in visiting the mothers, so the connection between the mothers and our work is kept close. We receive no opposition from the government authorities, and are constantly having children apply for entrance. Bible instruction is given through the telling of Bible stories, and Christian truth is made to underlie all of the work.*

Kyōtō Kindergartens.

These are two ; the Nishijin, and the Margaret Ayres. They are enjoying great prosperity, the latter having been spoken of as the best in the city. Four of the six efficient teachers are graduates of the Joshi Gakuin, " a fact that will bear repeating as long as they remain in the work where they have all been for several years." Thirty-three graduated from the two schools in March, after which there were more applicants than could be admitted. The number of graduates from the founding of the schools eight or ten years ago is two hundred and twelve ; the present enrollment is 95. The returns as an evangelizing agency may not be directly apparent, but no one may talk of christianizing Japan in the present generation who is not a sincere and active champion of Christian primary education in all its forms."†

Shinagawa Kindergarten.

A kindergarten of sixty pupils is reported at Shinagawa.§ In addition to the above, at least one girls-school has a

---

* Miss Mayo. † Miss Hawroth. § Mrs. MacNair.

kindergarten department, and there is no doubt other work of this kind not reported. In the kindergarten and Shō Gakkō work it is especially pleasing to note the degree to which the schools are simply the means to get into social relations with the parents. There is no doubt that worked carefully along these lines, the evangelizing efficiency of our present educational institutions can be increased fifty per cent.

Kanazawa Shō Gakkō.

* " The Primary and Secondary School for children in Kanazawa under the West Presbyterian Mission closed its doors with the annual commencement in March. The mission at first suggested its union with our Jo Gakkō here ; but upon investigating the situation, that course was not deemed advisable. The almost constant interference for the past three years of local officials, with lack of necessary missionary force to continue all lines of work combined with the great need of enlarging our kindergarten quarters, caused the mission to decide upon closing the Primary School. Although it was the only Christian school for children in the whole Hokurikudō, with our inability to offer sufficient attractions as a private school, and with government interference instead of assistance, we were unable to increase our numbers to any great extent, or to carry on the school successfully. The last year of the school life passed pleasantly. We were able to hold the forty-five pupils in the school until the last, and graduated three from the higher department. All of the older girls have entered the preparatory department of our Jo Gakko, while the older boys were given permission to enter the city Chū Gakkō, a privilege not granted for a number of years. One of the older boys was baptized in April. A number still come to the Sunday-school. So, though we cannot reach the children of this age daily, we hope to do all we can through the medium of the Sunday-school and the home. The children, from their knitting society and Christmas offering, contributed over twelve

---

* Miss Luther.

yen during the year for benevolent objects. We believe the school has accomplished much for the cause of Christ; and now though its doors are closed, and we may lose sight of many who have received instruction within its walls, the principles of Christianity have been planted in many hearts, and will tell in the future life of the boys and girls of this city."

Keimo Sho Gakko, Nos. 1 and 2 Tokyo.

*"The work under my care consists of two primary schools, instruction being carried in each through the Koto grades. In Keimo No. 1 Tsukiji, the entire number enrolled during the year was 135. Thirty-one left during the year. One hundred and four are with us at present, (March 31st). Of those who left, eight boys and five girls went out to service. Of the boys, one went to learn the carpenter's trade, seven to become errand boys, (kozo). The girls are engaged in making cigars and match boxes. Eight children were kept at home to work, and nine removed to another part of the city. Nine children completed the primary course. During the twenty-five years the school has been in existence, 145 have finished the course. The gain in numbers over last year has been thirty. Keimo No. 1, Shiba, graduated a class of twelve from the primary and one from the higher (Koto) department. The present number in that school is 105. During the twenty-five years of the existence of this school, 144 have completed the course. Among these we know of twelve who are Christians. The present higher class numbers twenty-nine. Since November, 1902 twenty-seven from the higher department have professed Christ. One of these has received baptism in the Shiba Church. We have formed them into a Junior Endeavor Society. A weekly meeting is held, and all take an active part. Their changed lives make the school a very different place."

Kiiku Sho Gakko. This is situated in Osaka and is in charge of Mrs. Winn. †"It has been very prosperous in

---

* Mrs. McCauley. † Mr. Winn.

attendance, the children filling the building to overflowing." It has one hundred and forty pupils and four teachers. Nineteen graduated this year.

CONCLUSION

With this our report comes to a close. Perhaps in describing our work, each of us unconsciously refers to that which has pleased him most, and possibly the editor has been similarly influenced in summing up the whole. Certainly we can each of us remember times during the year when our hearts have been as heavy as lead, and we have felt the work to be going backward rather than forward. But after making all due allowances, it must still remain that this has been a wonderful year; a year of the right hand of the Most High. We have received more than we have asked or thought. We have worked just as hard other years, but it is this year that the Lord has graciously permitted us to see much of the fruit of our own labors and of those who have toiled before us.

These things ought to make us very humble. Have we not each one of us at some time stood in the presence of mighty natural forces, before whose potency for good or ill we have felt oppressed and helpless, like little, very little, children? And as we stand in Japan to day, and by this year's experiences get a faint idea of what wonderful changes, what wonderful spiritual revolutions, the Spirit of God and he alone can work in a nation, must we not feel individually very humble, very helpless, and simply continue to pray, O Lord, Make bare thy mighty arm?

III

STATISTICAL TABLES

BY THE

Rev. H. M. Landis

The note below* appears in the Twenty-third Annual Report of the Council. It is repeated here as a general statement worthy of the attention of such friends of foreign missions as are particularly interested in the matter of statistics.

---

* The following tables, though prepared with much care and of real value, should not be relied upon as perfectly correct. The same is true of perhaps most tables of mission statistics; even the greatest painstaking and the multiplication of items do not secure entire accuracy. For their intelligent use the following also must be remembered: *a* In many cases it is not possible to *classify* with precision. For example: Two institutions, grouped together as schools, may differ widely in their work and requirements. *b* In different tables, especially in tables prepared in different mission fields, the same term may be used to describe things that are essentially different. For example: In one table, the term self-supporting church may be used in the same sense as at home; in another table, a group of Christians may be rated as a self supporting church, provided it receives no financial aid from the mission, though it has no pastor and dispenses with other aids to Christian life that call for Christian giving. *c* Tables of statistics deal only with *numbers*; they do not exhibit *quality*, which is of equal if not of greater importance. *d* Plausible but misleading inferences are easily drawn from such tables by one who has not a full knowledge and clear understanding of other facts and particularly of *reasons* which can not be tabulated. Of especial importance is it that these points be remembered by those who are interested in the study of mission work and the establishment of correct general principles for its conduct.

MISSION STATISTICS FOR 1902

MISSION OF THE	Missionaries					Stations			Educational work			
	Men			Women		Total including wives	Where missionaries reside	Out-stations	Theological schools	Students in same	Schools for Bible women	Students in same
	Married		Unmarried									
	Or-dained	Unor-dained	Or-dained	Unor-dained	Unmarried							
Pres. Church in U.S.A. (North)												
East Japan	7		1		13	29	5	? 24	½	6	1	17
West Japan	9		1		8	27	7	30			1	2
Total	16		1		21	56	12	54	½	6	2	19
Refd. (Dutch) Church in A.												
North Japan	5				5	17	5	18	½	6	1	5
South Japan	3		1		3	10	3	16				
Total	8		1		8	27	8	34	½	6	?	?
Pres. Church in U.S. (South)	11				8	30	9	27	½	6	?	?
Refd. (German) in U.S.	7		1		4	21	3	49	1	7	1	2
Cumberland Pres. Church	6		1		6	19	5	40				
Womans Union					6	6	1	5			1	28
Grand Total (1902-3)	48	3	4		53	159	38	209	2	25	? 5	54
Grand Total (1901-2)	45	2	3	1	55	153	38	234	3	24	6	63
Increase	3	1	1			6				1		
Decrease				1	2			25	1			

73

MISSION STATISTICS FOR 1902 (CONTINUED)

MISSION OF THE	Boys boarding schools	Pupils in same	Girls boarding schools	Pupils in same	Day (primary) schools	Pupils in same	Christian pupils of all schools	Uniting with the church during the year	Foreign teachers Men	Foreign teachers Women	Japanese teachers Men	Japanese teachers Women	Tuition
Pres. Church in U.S.A. (North)													
East Japan	½	115	2	355	5	472	233	57	2	12	20	33	4944
West Japan			3	130	5	339	36	11		8	13	33	1598
Total	½	115	5	485	10	811	269	68	2	20	31	53	6542
Refd. (Dutch) Church in A.													
North Japan	½	115	1	79			52	12	2	3	10	3	2452
South Japan	1	100	1	75			35	20	2	2	10	5	1170
Total	1½	215	2	154			57	32	4	5	20	8	3622
Pres. Church in U.S. (South)			1	60			25	5	2	2	3	5	450
Refd. (German) in U.S.	1	171	1	97			87	13	4	4	21	7	2216
Cumberland Pres. Church			1	92			?	?		3	3	3	484
Womans Union			1	89			40	15		26	4	8	364
Grand Total (1902-3)	3	501	11	977	10	811	478+	133+	10	40	84	97	13678
Grand Total (1901-2)	3	409	11	852	11	720	475+	149+	10	40	88	101	
Increase		92		125		91	3+	61+			4	4	
Decrease					1								

MISSION STATISTICS FOR 1902 (CONTINUED)

MISSION OF THE	Ed. wk. (con.) Granted by boards	Japanese ministers	Salaries of same	Itinerating expenses of same	Unordained preachers	Evangelistic work — Salaries of same	Itinerating expenses of same	Bible women	Salaries of same	Itinerating expenses of same	Granted by the Boards
Pres. Church in U.S.A. (North)											
East Japan	11230	6	1768	94	14	3261	440	17	1411	120	9366
West Japan	8034	8	2106	205	23	6277	771	8½	885	135+	12509+
Total	19264	14	3874	299	37	9538	1211	25½	2296	255+	21875+
Refd. (Dutch) Church in A.											
North Japan	6478	5	1500	500	11	2656	.	3	342	.	5902
South Japan	6600	3	1370	170	9	3384	420	1	144	10	7000
Total	13078	8	2870	670	20	6040	420	4	486	10	14902
Pres. Church in U.S. (South)	3750	4	†	500	18	5241	773	11	697	.	11000
Refd. (German) in U.S.	15500	8	2694	200	27	6225	800	13	1100	300	12800
Cumberland Pres. Church	6000	4	786	540	10	2460	516	0	804	113	5600
Womans Union	1142							27	3240	720	4800
Grand Total (1902-3)	58784	38	10222	1718	112	29504	3720	80½	8623	1398	71977
Grand Total (1901-2)	51996	§140	§39728	§5438				89	9020	1021	61587+
Increase	6788			1916				1½		377	11390
Decrease		1	4832						1297		

* All itinerating expenses reported under one column.
† Salaries of ministers reported under those of unordained preachers.
§ Ministers, unordained preachers, with salaries and itinerating expenses, reported together in 1901 as 141, 31886, 3522.

STATISTICS OF CHURCH OF CHRIST IN JAPAN FOR 1902

Presbytery	Total membership	Adult membership	Adult additions	Proportion of adult additions to adult membership	Sunday school membership (including teachers)	Proportion of S.S. members to adult church membership	Contributions to Board of Home Missions Yen	Contributions to all objects Yen	Average per Adult Member				Full members of Presbytery*
									Contributions to Home Missions		Contribution to all objects		
									1901	1902	1901	1902	
Tokyo	5680	5041	459	.0982	2867	.57	883.205	15203.523	.150	.175	3.78	3.02	34
Naniwa	3472	2909	259	.0890	1686	.58	480.800	12299.750	.159	.165	2.78	4.23	19
Miyagi	2153	2003	225	.1123	2677	1.34	167.121	4192.048	.078	.083	2.61	2.09	12
Sanyo	535	447	45	.1007	978	2.19	338.565	1810.353	.171	.757	3.04	4.05	5
Chinzei	631	493	51	.1035	2018	4.09	1107.220	1353.410	.203	2.266	2.47	2.75	4
Total	12471	10893	1075	.0987	10226	.94	2976.911	34859.084	.158	.273	3.19	3.20	74
Total for 1901	11750	10242	1213	.1194	8415	.83	1846.52	37180.57	For 1900 .122	For 1901 .158	For 1900 2.86	For 1901 3.19	84
Increase	721	651			1811	.11	1130.391		.036	.115		.01	9
Decrease			138	.0207				2321.486			.33		

*Including missionaries who have joined Presbyteries by letter

STATISTICS OF CHURCH OF CHRIST IN JAPAN FOR 1902 (CONTINUED)

PRESBYTERY	Advisory members of Presbytery †	Lay preachers ‡	Organized churches	Companies of believers	Total of two preceding items	Infant baptisms	Children included in total membership	Total Income including gifts Yen	Total expenditure Yen	Average per adult member Total Income 1902	Average per adult member Total Income 1901	Average per adult member Total expenditure 1902	Average per adult member Total expenditure 1901	Gifts mainly or altogether from missions Yen	Average per adult member for gifts 1901	Average per adult member for gifts 1902
Tokyo	4	36	35	33	68	51	639	17880.674	17498.229	3.55	4.93	3.47	4.75	2677.151	1.15	.53
Naniwa	15	22	17	29	46	57	563	16609.600	14825.960	5.71	4.68	5.19	4.99	4309.850	1.94	1.48
Miyagi	9	12	8	27	35	32	150	9798.550	9733.069	4.89	6.10	4.86	5.96	5606.502	3.49	2.80
Sanyo	3	7	7	7	14	4	88	4659.036	4324.444	10.43	8.53	9.67	6.76	2849.583	5.19	6.37
Chinzei	5	11	7	10	17	15	138	5850.880	5627.860	11.87	10.04	11.42	10.01	4497.470	7.57	9.12
Total	36	88	74	106	180	159	1578	54799.640	52009.562	5.03		4.77		19940.556	2.20	1.83
Total for 1901	33	90	71	108	179	145	1508	56577.69	54041.29	5.32		5.32		17550.60		2.20
Increase	3		3		1	14	70			.29				2389.956		
Decrease		2		2				1778.05	2031.728			.55				.37

† For the sake of missionaries coöperating with the Church of Christ in Japan, but who are unable to enter Presbyteries in the usual way by letters of dismission from the other Presbyteries, the following provision is made:—Canon 21 § 6. Advisory Members: Ministers who sincerely accept the Constitution, Canons and Confession of Faith, and who statedly coöperate in the work of the Church of Christ in Japan, but who are unable to supply for admission under Canon 14, may be admitted as Advisory Members by a two-thirds vote. Advisory Members may speak, introduce resolutions, and be elected to serve on committees; but no committee shall have a majority of Advisory Members. Presbyteries having four or less than four Advisory Members shall elect one to sit as an Advisory Member of the Synod. Those having eight shall elect two; those having twelve, three.

‡ Lay-preachers are men regularly licensed by a Presbytery to preach the gospel. They shall labor under the direction of the Presbytery, or of such ministers as the Presbytery shall appoint, to their oversight. Constitution, Art. 7.

§ As here employed, the term means companies of baptized believers not yet organized as churches, but under the direct care of a Presbytery and whose names are enrolled in a register kept by the Clerk of the Presbytery. Canon 1.

STATISTICS OF PRESBYTERIES FOR 1902 COMPARED WITH THOSE FOR 1901

Presbyteries		Membership Jan. 1st, 1902				Increase											
						Baptized			Restored			Recd. from other Churches			Transfers from churches of other Pres.		
		M	W	C	Total	M	W	C	M	W	C	M	W	C	M	W	C
Tokyo	Churches	1900	1949	485	4334	241	161	32	9	8	3	35	23	6	33	24	15
	Pr Pl.*	435	388	132	955	37	32	19	13	3	1	4	2	1	1	4	
	Total	2335	2337	617	5289	278	193	51	22	11	4	39	25	7	34	28	15
Naniwa	Churches	1010	1084	405	2499	127	74	38	1			8	10	4	18	14	4
	Pr. Pl.	386	328	125	839	27	21	19	1			7	3	1	2	6	4
	Total	1396	1412	530	3338	154	95	57	2			15	13	5	20	20	8
Miyagi	Churches	536	409	51	996	46	48	7	3	4			1		5	6	1
	Pr. Pl.	569	340	70	979	90	38	25	2			6	5	5	10	7	1
	Total	1105	749	121	1975	136	86	32	5	4		6	6	5	15	13	
Sanyo	Churches	147	174	80	401	19	5	1	1			4	9		7	9	
	Pr. Pl.	48	50	21	119	12	4	3				2				2	
	Total	195	224	101	520	31	9	4	1			6	9		7	11	
Chinzei	Churches	177	166	107	450	23	8	12	1	1		1		1			
	Pr. Pl.	76	70	32	178	10	6	3	1			1	2		3	4	
	Total	253	236	139	628	33	14	15	2	1		5	2	2	3	4	
	G. Total	5284	4958	1508	11750	632	397	159	32	16	4	71	55	18	79	76	24

* Unorganized churches.

STATISTICS FOR PRESBYTERIES FOR 1902 (COMPARED WITH THOSE FOR 1901 (CONTINUED)

Presbyteries		Increase (cont.) Transfers from churches of same Presbytery			Confirmations		Dismissals To churches of same Presbytery			Decrease To churches of other Presbyteries			Dismissed to other Churches			Deaths		
		M	W	C	M	W	M	W	C	M	W	C	M	W	C	M	W	C
Tokyo	Churches	31	32	10	14	8	24	32	12	22	28	15	19	20	1	21	26	5
	Pr. Pl. *	4	14	2		2	10	9		3	1		2	2		15	8	
	Total	35	46	12	14	10	34	41	12	25	29	15	21	22	1	36	34	5
Naniwa	Churches	47	47	6	1	8	30	37	11	25	23		14	10		13	9	
	Pr. Pl.	26	37	14		1	18	28	7	5	4	4				4	5	3
	Total	73	84	20	1	9	48	65	18	30	27	4	14	10		17	14	3
Miyagi	Churches	6	3	2		1	12	5	2	9	2		5	7		2	5	
	Pr. Pl.	15	7	4	2		10	6	2	11			5	1	1	6	3	
	Total	21	10	6	2	1	22	11	2	20	2		10	8	1	8	8	
Sanyo	Churches	4	4		2	3	5	9	3	10	8	6	1	5	3	1	1	
	Pr. Pl.	1	1	5	2	3	1				1						1	
	Total	5	5	5	2	3	6	9	3	10	9	6	1	5	3	1	2	
Chinzei	Churches	2	1	2	2	2	17	8	4	11	15	4	2	4		1	5	1
	Pr. Pl.	3	2				1			1							3	
	Total	5	3	2	2	2	18	8	4	12	15	4	2	4		3	8	1
	G. Total	139	118	45	21	25	128	134	39	97	82	29	48	49	6	66	66	9

* Unorganized churches.

STATISTICS OF PRESBYTERIES FOR 1902 COMPARED WITH THOSE FOR 1901 (CONTINUED)

PRESBYTERIES		Decrease (Con.)					Resident elsewhere			Special Items						Membership Jan. 1st, 1903		
		Exclusions		Names dropped from Registers						Debarred from communion		Lost trace of						
		M	W	M	W	C	M	W	C	M	W	M	W	C	M	W	C	Total
Tokyo	Churches	5	3	65	34	9	676	569	134	16	11	95	66	8	2107	2062	487	4656
	Pr. Pl. *		1	9	7	1	112	79	18	7	3	5	9	2	455	417	152	1024
	Total	5	4	74	41	10	788	648	152	23	14	100	75	10	2562	2479	639	5680
Naniwa	Churches	6		16	13	7	367	334	72	1	2	5	3		1111	1147	427	2685
	Pr. Pl.			1			121	104	42			9	3		342	309	136	787
	Total	6		17	13	7	488	438	114	1	2	14	6		1453	1456	563	3472
Miyagi	Churches	3	1	35	12		190	131	20	10	2	12	9		533	428	47	1008
	Pr. Pl.			3	4		244	135	32	5	4	9	4	2	662	380	103	1145
	Tota	3	1	38	16		434	266	52	15	6	21	13	2	1195	808	150	2153
Sanyo	Churches			6	8	5	43	42	26			17	10	3	160	171	59	390
	Pr. Pl.						11	13	3			10	6		61	55	29	145
	Total			6	8	5	54	55	29			27	16	3	221	226	88	535
Chinzei	Churches			3	3	7	55	47	3	1	1	1			173	143	102	418
	Pr. Pl.						20	20	10						98	79	36	213
	Total			3	3	7	75	67	42	1	1	1			271	222	138	631
	G. Total	14	5	138	81	29	1839	1474	389	40	23	163	110	15	5702	5191	1578	12471

* Unorganized churches.

STATISTICS OF PRESBYTERIES FOR 1902 COMPARED WITH THOSE FOR 1901 (CONTINUED)

PRESBYTERIES		Attendance at communion	Average attendance at Sunday services		Av. at. at prayer meeting		Sunday Schools									Income		
							Children		Adults		Average attendance		Teachers		Offerings		Miscellaneous	
			M	W	M	W	M	W	M	W	M	W	M	W				
Tokyo	Churches	2695	724	610	293	194	781	909	120	137	540	777	74	65	13141	118	304	475
	Pr. Pl. *	591	208	165	125	93	275	368	47	42	227	297	28	21	1757	930		
	Total	3286	932	775	418	287	1056	1277	167	179	767	1076	102	86	14899	48	304	475
Naniwa	Churches	1546	460	424	216	158	293	369	168	133			41	55	9836	530	226	770
	Pr. Pl.	409	193	195	104	110	182	206	90	86			30	33	2129	690	106	760
	Total	1955	653	619	320	268	475	575	258	219			71	88	11966	220	333	530
Miyagi	Churches	645	216	167	74	52	302	361	112	90	225	196	26	21	2500	428	255	224
	Pr. Pl.	623	267	158	115	74	796	862	22	12	494	408	43	30	1354	936	82	460
	Total	1268	483	325	189	126	1098	1223	134	102	719	604	69	51	3854	364	337	684
Sanyo	Churches	219	105	88	43	29	190	456	34	39	61	80	10	10	1496	252	63	898
	Pr. Pl.	76	50	30	27	16	77	78	40	29	69	72	8	7	248	667	1	536
	Total	295	155	118	70	45	267	534	74	68	130	152	18	17	1744	919	65	434
Chinzei	Churches	203	96	76	61	55	88	116	67	44	166	154	21	13	747	690	149	750
	Pr. Pl.	137	55	46	35	27	860	1005	74	193	100	107	12	6	421	460	34	510
	Total	340	151	122	96	82	948	1121	660	237	166	261	33	19	1169	150	184	260
	G. Total	7144	2374	1959	1093	808	3844	4730	1293	805	1882	2093	293	261	33633	701	1225	2383

* Unorganized churches.

81

STATISTICS OF PRESBYTERIES FOR 1902 COMPARED WITH THOSE FOR 1901 (CONTINUED)

PRESBYTERIES		Income (sen.?) Totals	Comparison with previous year		Receipts from Dendo Kyoku or Missions	Expenses				
			Increase	Decrease		Salary of pastor or evangelist	Charity	Contributions to Dendo Kyoku	Running expenses	
Tokyo	Churches	13445	1229 744	3412 395	910	6363 299	108 458	651 310	4972 771
	Pr. Pl. *	1757	930 335	456 1642 733	1767 151	1679 911	36 600	231 895	1154 316
	Total	15203	523 1565	2005 5055 128	2677 151	8043 210	145 58	883 205	6127 87
Naniwa	Churches	10063	200 2993	451 593 820	391 310	4280 480	146 490	394 210	2197 130
	Pr. Pl.	2236	450 590	390 583 90	3918 540	3542 500	17 570	86 590	1193 30
	Total	12299	750 3584	740 1686 910	4309 850	7822 980	164 60	480 800	3390 160
Miyagi	Churches	2755	652 78	890 184 212	873	2204	58 640	72 771	889 411
	Pr. Pl.	1437	396 435	632 722 258	4733 502	4442 500	42 626	94 350	1164 164
	Total	4192	48 513	522 908 470	5606 502	6646 500	101 266	167 121	2053 575
Sanyo	Churches	1560	150 231	522	441	830 900	1	257 925	521 867
	Pr. Pl.	250	203 59	203	2408 583	1701 500	22 940	80 610	551 985
	Total	1810	353 290	725 108 83	2849 583	2532 400	23 940	338 565	1073 825
Chinzei	Churches	897	440 81		1386 220	1625 400	34	409 240	79 270
	Pr. Pl.	455	970 130	190	3111 250	2484	8	697 980	116 710
	Total	1353	410 211	190	4497 470	4109 400	42 360	1107 220	195 980
G. Total		34859	846175	3777 7158 591	19940 556	29154 490	476 684	2976 911	12840 654

* Unorganized churches.

82

STATISTICS OF PRESBYTERIES FOR 1902 COMPARED WITH THOSE FOR 1901 (CONTINUED)

PRESBYTERIES		Expenses (yen)			Property						Deacons		Licentiates	Corresponding members	Churches organized	Companies of believers not or. as churches	Total
		Occasional expenses	Totals	Estimated value of ch. building manse land	Endowment	Preaching place	Elders	M	W	Ordained ministers						
Tokyo	Churches	1843	13030	5801	34618	3199	504	14	123	58	27			35		68
	Pr. Pl. *	455	3558	649	8795	38	380	14	47				436		33	
	Total	2299	17408	2293	43413	3237	884	28	170	58	27	34				
Naniwa	Churches	1669	8688	60	39302	1450	230	17	59	24	12			17		46
	Pr. Pl.	1298	6137	900	6330	366	930	20				19	22		29	
	Total	2967	14825	960	45732	1757	160	43	59				15			
Miyagi	Churches	420	3645	712	13154	217	800	6	28	22	12			8		35
	Pr. Pl.	343	6087	357	8650	834		18				12	912		27	
	Total	764	9733	69	22104	1051	800	24	28	22	5					
Sanyo	Churches	345	1956	764	6114	214		7	14	4	3			7		14
	Pr. Pl.	10	2367	680				7	14	4	3	5	3		7	
	Total	355	4324	444	6114	214		8	16	5	2					
Chinzei	Churches	68	2216	730	4970			7	14	4	3			7		17
	Pr. Pl.	104	3411	130	865			7	16	5	2	4	5		10	
	Total	172	5627	860	5655	870		15	16	5	2		11			
	G. Total	6560	52009	5622	23018	7107	130	844	171	287	113	49	74	36,88	74	106	180

* Unorganized churches.

83

IV

PRIVILEGES OBTAINED

FROM THE

DEPARTMENT OF EDUCATION

BY

MEIJI GAKUIN AND OTHER SCHOOLS

In the last Annual Report of the Council (pages 16-20) will be found an account of renewed efforts to obtain from the Department of Education for Meiji Gakuin and other similar Christian schools the privileges accorded to Chu Gakko (Middle Schools forming a part of the government system of education). Since the publication of that Report marked progress has been made. In order however to make the present situation clear to those who are not familiar with the past, the following quotation from the last Report is here inserted :—

" Those who have followed the history of Christian work in Japan during recent years will remember that in 1899 there was issued under the authority of the Minister of Education what it known as Instruction No. 12 ; an order which forbade all teaching of religion and all religious services in schools having government recognition. This forced all those who hold to the principle that schools carried on by Christian missions should be Christian institutions, to surrender government recognition along with its attendant privileges. After long and earnest efforts, while Instruction No. 12 was allowed to stand unchanged, regulations were issued by which the graduates of such schools as Meiji Gakuin were allowed precisely the same privileges as the graduates of the Chu Gakko, though the schools were not allowed to bear the name (Chu Gakko).

That concession on the part of the Department of Education was understood to be and was accepted as a final settlement of the question; but during the spring of this year (1902) new regulations were issued requiring the graduates of all schools excepting the Chu Gakko to pass a *special* examination, in *addition* to the examination required of the graduates of the Chu Gakko, in order to enter the Koto Gakko (High Schools). Also a special fee of 5 *yen* was to be paid for this special and preliminary examination.

Shortly after these new regulations were issued, Messrs. Ibuka, Honda, and Kataoka laid the case before the authorities and endeavored to obtain relief. Also a letter was addressed to the Minister of Education, signed by representives of Meiji Gakuin, Aoyama Gakuin, Tohoku Gakuin, and Doshisha. The letter was designed to bring the matter to the attention of Baron Kikuchi from the point of view of foreigners deeply interested in the welfare of the institutions affected by the regulations; and as it presents a somewhat full statement of the case it is inserted below.*

---

* To His Excellency Baron Dairoku Kikuchi.
Dear Baron Kikuchi:

We beg leave to address you as American missionaries representing a large number of Christians in America, who are deeply interested in Meiji Gakuin, Aoyama Gakuin, Tohoku Gakuin, Doshisha, and similar institutions in Japan.

About a year ago regulations were issued under which the graduates of such schools as these were permitted to enter Koto Gakko on precisely the same terms as the graduates of Chu Gakko: a privilege long hoped for and

Some time after the presentation of this letter to the Minister of Education, information was received that it would not be possible at the time to comply with the request. Dr. Ibuka and Mr. Honda therefore decided to make an attempt to obtain relief in another direction. In this they were successful.

There are in Japan what are known as Semmon Gakko: i.e. schools in which instruction is given in some particular branch of knowledge; and numbering in all a dozen or

highly prized. Recently however this privilege has been seriously curtailed by a new set of regulations. Before applying for permission to pass the competitive examination for admission to Koto Gakko, the graduates of these schools must first pass a special preliminary examination on all the subjects included in the Chu Gakko curriculum.

To the students who have just graduated from these schools, as well as to those who have entered upon the last year of the course and who can not now without difficulty change their school connection, this is a real hardship. It is also a manifest injury to the schools themselves. Last year their graduates had the same privileges as those of Chu Gakko; now they have not the same. But there is another point which we beg leave to urge upon your consideration. The regulations issued last year had a history behind them; they were the result of a long series of negotiations.

In 1898 what is known as Instruction No. 12 was issued under the sanction of the Minister of Education. Prior to that time a number of the schools above mentioned had been granted Chu Gakko licenses; but as Instruction No. 12 forbade all religious instruction and services, "even outside the regular course instruction," they were forced to surrender such licenses. This was because the funds by which these schools were founded, and with which they had been carried on, had been given upon the distinct understanding that they were always to be Christian institutions. Under these circumstances to retain their licenses would have been to betray their trust.

In the hope of obtaining relief a petition was presented to the Minister of Education. The Minister of Education, the Minister of Foreign Affairs, the Prime Minister, all kindly gave interviews to the petitioners; and when it appeared improbable that the original petition could be acceded to, another request was submitted. This was essentially the same plan as that embodied in the regulations issued last year; and regarding this the Minister of Education stated that he thought that in time it might be accepted. Months passed; from time to time inquiry was made; the information received gave grounds for continued hope. At last the regulations of last year were issued.

In view of all this, those in charge of these schools thought they had good reason for believing that the position of the schools, upon compliance with such instructions as the Department of Education might see fit to

more. Among them are the Commercial College, the Foreign Languages School, the Agricultural College at Sapporo, one or more Polytechnic Schools, and five or six Schools of Medicine. All of these Semmon Gakko are included in the government system of education; prepare students for a profession without the necessity of their passing through the University; and are in fact the schools which a considerable number of the

give, would be assured. The schools were visited by inspectors, and whatever changes or additions were declared necessary were cheerfully made. The new conditions were made public, and thereupon the number of students rapidly increased. The friends of the schools in America were informed of the new state of things, and preparations were making for the improvement of the schools. In one case, for example, the annual grant of funds for current expenses was increased by eight hundred *yen*; and fifteen thousand *yen* which had been held in trust until the prospects of the school should warrant their expenditure, were granted for the erection of a new building.

Taking all these facts into consideration, you will not we think regard it strange that the issuing of the recent regulation was a cause of very great disappointment and surprise; and we beg of you most earnestly to form some plan which shall restore to such schools as these the privileges granted last year after so much effort.

Reference has been made to Instruction No. 12. If that Instruction could be restricted in its application to schools supported by public funds, it would then be possible for the schools which we represent to become Chu Gakko; and that would render any special arrangement on their behalf unnecessary. No, doubt directly after the Instruction was issued, there were great difficulties in the way of such a restriction; but it has been our constant hope that the time would come when those difficulties would be no longer insuperable. We trust that that time is now approaching.

In conclusion we may be permitted to express what is our firm conviction on two points.

1 We believe that such schools as these, if only they receive such kindly encouragement as the Department of Education may properly afford them, will establish themselves as permanent institutions of great value to Japan in the education of her boys and young men.

2 We believe also that the restriction of Instruction No. 12 to such schools as are supported by *public* funds; and the granting to such schools as are supported by *private* funds, but which are recognized as doing the work of Chu Gakko, the rank of Chu Gakko together with the right of religious freedom in education, would do more than is commonly supposed still further to strengthen the feeling of friendship for Japan already so strong in England and America.

graduates of Meiji Gakuin and similar institutions wish to enter.

Until recently the regulations for admission to these Semmon Gakko permitted only the following classes of students to enter:—

1 Those who should pass the examination required by the institution to which application for entrance was made.

2 Graduates of Chu Gakko, Shihan Gakko (Normal Schools), and Koto Jo Gakko (High Schools for young women).

3 Those who had passed the examination for entrance to the Koto Gakko (High Schools for young men).

After much persevering and patient endeavor, Dr. Ibuka and Mr. Honda succeeded in having the following added to the regulations:—" Graduates of schools recognized by the Minister of Education as equal or superior to Chu Gakko."

The first Christian schools to obtain such recognition were Meiji Gakuin and Aoyama Gakuin. Subsequently it was obtained by Doshisha and Tohoku Gakuin. It has also been granted to the Chuto Kwa (Middle Department) of Gakushuin (Nobles School), and to two or three Buddhist institutions.

As already stated, the request presented to the Minister of Education that graduates of Meiji Gakuin and similar schools be allowed to enter Koto Gakko on precisely the same terms as graduates of Chu Gakko has not yet been granted; but that privilege would seem logically to follow the one now conceded. For these reasons: (1) The grade of scholarship required for admission to Koto Gakko is identical with that required for admission to Semmon Gakko. (2) As Semmon Gakko no less than Koto Gakko form a part of the government system of education, the principle hitherto followed by the Department of Education has evidently ceased to be controlling. Besides these reasons for encouragement another is to be found in the advice given to Dr. Ibuka and Mr. Honda. They were advised to allow the matter of entrance to Koto Gakko to rest for the present, as it is the intention of the Department to change the name Koto Gakko to Daigaku Yobimon (Preparatory Schools to the University), and as with that change these will be certain changes in the regulations.

V

BOARD OF MISSIONS
OF THE
CHURCH OF CHRIST IN JAPAN
(DENDO KYOKU)

The work of the Board of Missions of the Church of Christ in Japan is under the general direction of the Synod, and is carried on independently of the Council of Missions. It is however a work in whose success the Council is deeply interested; and an account of it may properly form a part of the Annual Report of the Council. The following report for 1902 was prepared by Mr. Landis, to whom the Council is indebted for much other statistical work.

PLACES UNDER THE CARE OF THE BOARD OF MISSIONS, WITH THE NAMES OF PASTORS OR EVANGELISTS IN CHARGE

Formosa (Taihoku, Tainan, Taichu), Messrs. Kawai, Shimamura, Hosokawa; Hiroshima, Mr. Shirai; Isezaki, Mr. Tominaga; Kumamoto, Mr. Oishi; Mito, Mr. Kuwada; Okayama, Mr. Hoshino; Tokyo (Hamacho, Hongo, Yotsuya), Messrs. Tonomura, Arima, Wada; Yokosuka, Mr. Akimoto.

RECEIPTS FROM

	Yen
Places under the care of the Board of Missions.*	826.162
Presbyteries of the Church of Christ in Japan.†	1624.868
Societies et cetera connected with Church.‡	339.732
Missions coöperating with the Church of Christ in Japan. (The English Presbyterian Mission in Formosa contributed yen 50. Besides this in certain places work formerly carried on by missions has been turned over to the Board which receives from the missions the same amount of funds formerly expended by them in those places)§	454.50
Individual Missionaries	428.10
„ Japanese ministers	195.87
„ Japanese church members.	1283.322
	5152.554

DISBURSEMENTS

	Yen
Salaries of pastors and evangelists.	3356.24
Itinerating of evangelists	373.60
Expenses for evangelistic work	74.061
Office expenses	350.015
Rent	428.
Postage et cetera	122.975
Printing	103.30
Incidental	328.05
Interest	16.
Balance	.313
	5152.554

* Tainan, 3; Hiroshima, 182.316; Isezaki, 180; Kumamoto, 68; Mito, 67; Okayama, 63.80; Hamacho, 2.295; Hongo, 68.25; Yotsuya, 74.141; Yokosuka, 107.36; Awamizu, 7; Kuji, 3. Total 826.162.

† Tokyo, 667.401; Miyagi, 236.864; Naniwa, 483.011; Sanyo, 132.410; Chinzei, 105.182. Total 1624.868.

‡ Womens Societies, 107.081; Sunday-schools, 14.241; Young Peoples Societies, 11.575; girls-schools, 20.06; other donors, 186.775. Total 339.732.

§ East Japan Presbyterian Mission, 390; West Japan Presbyterian Mission, 4.50; Cumberland Presbyterian Mission 10; English Presbyterian Mission in Formosa, 50. Total 454.50.

CONTRIBUTIONS FROM PRESBYTERIES INCLUDING THOSE FROM SOCIETIES AND INDIVIDUALS

Tokyo	Churches	1149.023	
	Preaching-places	128.988	1278.011
Miyagi	Churches	164.777	
	Preaching-places	207.175	371.952
Naniwa	Churches	749.576	
	Preaching-places	142.674	892.250
Sanyo	Churches	201.511	
	Preaching-places	26.696	228.207
Chinzei	Churches	97.12	
	Preaching-places	51.362	148.482
			2918.902

CONTRIBUTIONS FORM INDIVIDUAL CHURCH MEMBERS ACCORDING TO DISTRICTS

Tokyo	552.066
Yokohama	105.90
Hokkaido	88.655
Tohoku	19.921
Tokaido	56.10
Hokurikudo	18.50
Shikoku	80.68
Chikoku	103.97
Kwanto Shinetsu	47.65
Kyūshū	88.95
Kinai	106.90
Formosa	14.03
	1283.322

The following six churches contributed over one hundred yen each: viz. Ichi Bancho (Tokyo), Nihonbashi (Tokyo), Kaigan (Yokohama), Kobe, Kochi, Akamagaseki. Twelve churches contributed between fifty and one hundred yen each: viz. Shiba (Tokyo), Ichigaya (Tokyo), Daimachi (Tokyo), Shiloh (Yokohama), Osaka

East, Osaka West, Osaka North, Osaka South, Nagoya Otaru, Sapporo, Taihoku (Formosa).

The number of individual donors contributing directly to the Board was 368; an increase of 148 over the previous year. Of these, 52 were Japanese ministers; 37 were missionaries; and 279 church members. Three contributed one hundred *yen* or more; three, from fifty to one hundred; fifteen, from twenty to fifty; fifteen, from eleven to fifteen: twenty, ten; fifty-six, from five to ten; and the rest (256) something less than five each.

COMPARISON OF RECEIPTS WITH THOSE OF THE PREVIOUS YEAR

	1901	1902	Increase and decrease
Places under the care of the Board	861.019	826.462	− 34.557
Presbyteries	981.359	1624.868	+ 643.609
Societies and missions	322.491	794.232	+ 471.741
Individuals	743.299	1907.292	+ 1163.993
Special		133.400	+ 133.400
	2908.168	5286.254	+ 2378.086

SIMILAR COMPARISON OF RECEIPTS FROM PRESBYTERIES

	1901	1902	Increase
Tokyo	415.980	667.401	251.421
Miyagi	113.813	236.864	123.052
Naniwa	315.054	483.011	167.917
Sanyo	67.440	132.410	64.970
Chinzei	69.033	105.182	36.149
	981.359	1624.868	643.509

RECEIPTS OF BOARD FROM THE FORMATION OF THE PRESENT ORGANIZATION

1894	207.702
1895	1021.438
1896	1620.419
1897	2629.939
1898	2791.251
1899	2759.042
1900	3416.452
1901	2908.168
1902	5286.254
	22635.665

VI
ROLL OF THE COUNCIL

EAST JAPAN MISSION OF THE PRESBYTERIAN CHURCH IN THE U.S.A. (NORTHERN)

Ballagh, Mr. J.C., 1875†	. . . .	Tokyo
Ballagh, Mrs. J.C., 1884 .	. in U.S.	,,
Haworth, Rev. B.C., D.D., 1887	. .	,,
Haworth, Mrs. B.C. .	. . . .	,,
Imbrie, Rev. William, D.D., 1875	. .	,,
Imbrie, Mrs. William,	. . . .	,,
Johnson, Rev. W.T., 1902.	. . .	Sapporo
Johnson, Mrs. W.T.,.	. . . .	,,
Landis, Rev. H.M., 1888 .	. . .	Tokyo
Landis, Mrs. H.M. .	. . . .	,,
MacNair, Rev. T.M., 1883	. . .	,,
MacNair, Mrs. T.M., 1880	. . .	,,
Pierson, Rev. G.P., 1888 .	. . .	Asahigawa
Pierson, Mrs. G.P., 1891 .	. . .	,,
Thompson, Rev. David, D.D., 1863 .	.	Tokyo
Thompson, Mrs. David, 1873 .	. .	,,
Alexander, Miss Emma, 1902 .	. .	Tokyo
Ballagh, Miss A.P., 1884 .	. in U.S.	,,
Gardner, Miss Sarah, 1889	. ,, ,, .	Tokyo

† Year of arrival in Japan as missionary.

McCauley, Mrs. J.K., 1880	. . .	Tokyo
Milliken, Miss Elizabeth P., 1884	. .	,,
Rose, Miss C.H., 1886	. . .	Otaru
Sherman, Miss Mary Belle, 1902	. .	Sapporo
Smith, Miss S.C., 1880	. . . .	,,
Ward, Miss Isabel Mae, 1901,	. . .	,,
West, Miss A.B., 1883	. . . .	Tokyo
Wyckoff, Miss Helena, 1901	. . .	,,
Youngman, Miss K.M. 1873	. . .	,,

WEST JAPAN MISSION OF THE PRESBYTERIAN CHURCH IN THE U.S.A. (NORTHERN)

Ayres, Rev. J.B., 1888* ,	. . .	Yamaguchi
Ayres, Mrs. J.B.,*	. . . . .	,,
Brokaw, Rev. H., 1896	. . .	Hiroshima
Brokaw, Mrs. H.,	. . . . .	,,
Bryan, Rev. A.V., 1882*	. . . .	Matsuyama
Bryan, Mrs. A.V., 1887*	. . . .	,,
Curtis, Rev. F.S., 1887	. . . .	Kyoto
Curtis, Mrs. F.S.,	. . . . .	,,
Dunlop, Rev. J.G., 1890*	. . . .	Fukui
Dunlop, Mrs. J.G., 1894	. . . .	,,
Erdman, Rev. J.P., 1903*.	. . .	Yamaguchi
Fulton, Rev. G.W., 1889	. . . .	Kanazawa
Fulton, Mrs. G.W.,	. . . .	,,
Jones, Rev. W.Y., 1895*	. . in U.S.	Fukui
Jones, Mrs. W.Y., 1884	. . ,, ,, .	,,
Langsdorf, Rev. W.B., Ph.D., Litt.D., 1902*.		Hiroshima
Langsdorf, Mrs. W.B.,*	. . . .	,,
Murray, Rev. D.A., D.D., 1902*	. .	Osaka
Winn, Rev. T.C., 1878*	. . . .	,,
Winn, Mrs. T.C.,*	. . . .	,,
Bigelow, Miss G.S., 1886	. . in U.S.	Yamaguchi
Cooper, Miss Mary B., 1903	. . .	Hiroshima
Foster, Miss A.L.A., 1902.	. . .	Yamaguchi
Garvin, Miss A.E., 1882	. . in U.S.	Osaka

* Present at meeting of Council in Arima, September, 1903.

Gibbons, Miss K. Anna, 1902*	. . .	Kanazawa
Haworth, Miss Alice, 1888	. . .	Kyoto
Jones, Miss Anna W., 1903	. . .	Osaka
Luther, Miss Ida R., 1898.	. . .	Kanazawa
Mayo, Miss Lucy E. 1901.	. . .	,,
Palmer, Miss M.M., 1892 .	. . .	Yamaguchi
Shaw, Miss Kate, 1889	. . in U.S.	Kanazawa
Wells, Miss Lillian, 1900 .	. . .	Matsuyama

NORTH JAPAN MISSION OF THE REFORMED
(DUTCH) CHURCH IN AMERICA

Ballagh, Rev. J. H., 1861 .	. . .	Yokohama
Ballagh, Mrs. J. H. .	. . .	,,
Booth, Rev. Eugene S., 1879	. . .	,,
Booth, Mrs. Eugene S.	. . .	,,
Harris, Rev. Howard, 1883	. . .	Aomori
Harris, Mrs. Howard,	. . .	,,
Miller, Rev. E. Rothesay, 1872.	. .	Tokyo
Miller, Mrs. E. Rothesay, 1870.	. .	,,
Oltmans, Rev. A., D.D., 1886 .	. .	Nagano
Oltmans, Mrs. A.	. . .	,,
Scudder, Rev. Frank S., 1897 .	in U.S.	,,
Scudder, Mrs. Frank S.	. . ,, ,, .	,,
Wyckoff, M. N., D. Sc, 1881 .	. .	Tokyo
Wyckoff, Mrs. M. N.	. . .	,,
Deyo, Miss Mary, 1888* .	. . .	Morioka
Moulton, Miss Julia, 1891 .	. . .	,,
Schenck, Mrs. J. W., 1897	. in U.S.	Nagano
Thompson, Miss Anna De F., 1887 .	.	Yokohama
Winn, Miss L., 1881*	. . . .	Morioka
Wyckoff, Miss Harriet J , 1898 .	. .	Yokohama

SOUTH JAPAN MISSION OF THE REFORMED
(DUTCH) CHURCH IN AMERICA

Hondelink, Rev. Garret, 1903 .	. .	
Myers, Rev. C. M., 1899 .	. . .	Nagasaki
Peeke, Rev. H. V. S., 1888*	. . .	Saga

Peeke, Mrs. H. V. S.	Saga
Pieters, Rev. Albertus, 1891* . . .	Kumamoto
Pieters, Mrs, Albertus . . , .	,,
Stout, Rev. Henry, D.D., 1869* . .	Nagasaki
Couch, Miss Sara M., 1892* .	Nagasaki
Hoekje, Miss Grace, 1903. .	Kagoshima
Lansing, Miss H. M., 1893* .	,,
Stout, Miss A. B., 1898* . .	Nagasaki

MISSION OF THE PRESBYTERIAN CHURCH
IN THE U.S. (SOUTHERN)

Buchanan, Rev. W. C., 1891* . . .	Takamatsu
Buchanan, Mrs. W. C.	,,
Buchanan, Rev. Walter, McS., 1895 in U.S.	,,
Buchanan, Mrs. Walter, McS., 1887 ,, ,, .	,,
Cumming, Rev. C. K., 1889* . . .	Gifu
Cumming, Mrs. C. K., 1892* . . .	,,
Fulton, Rev. S. P., D.D., 1888* . .	Tokyo
Fulton, Mrs. S. P.*	,,
Hope, Rev. S. R., 1892*	Toyohashi
Hope, Mrs. S. R.*	,,
Johnson, Mr. Cameron, (Associate Member)	Kobe
Johnson, Mrs. Cameron, ,, ,,	,,
Logan, Rev. C. A., 1902	Tokushima
Logan, Mrs. C. A.*	,,
McAlpine, Rev. R. E., 1885* . in U.S.	Nagoya
McAlpine, Mrs. R. E. . . ,, ,,	,,
McIlwaine, Rev. W. B., 1889* . . .	Kochi
McIlwaine, Mrs. W. B.*	,,
Moore, Rev. J. W., 1890*. . . .	Susaki
Moore, Mrs. J. W., 1893*. . . .	,,
Myers, Rev. H. W., 1897* . . .	Tokushima
Myers, Mrs. H. W.*	,,
Price, Rev. H. B., 1887*	Kobe
Price, Mrs. H. B., 1890	,,
Atkinson, Miss Maria, 1899* . .	
Dowd, Miss Annie, 1888 . in U.S.	Kochi

Evans, Miss Sala, 1893*		Nagoya
Houston, Miss Ella, 1891		,,
Moore, Miss Elizabeth, 1894 .	in U.S.	,,
Patton Miss A. V., 1900*		Tokushima
Patton, Miss Florence, 1895 .	in U.S.	,,
Sterling, Miss Charlotte E., 1888 . .		Kochi

MISSION OF THE REFORMED (GERMAN) CHURCH IN THE U.S.

Cook, Mr. H. H., 1902		Sendai
Faust, Rev. A. K., 1900		,,
Faust, Mrs. A. K., 1903		,,
Gerhard, Rev. Paul L., 1897 . . .		,,
Gerhard, Mrs. Paul L., 1902 . . .		,,
Lampe, Rev. W. E., 1900 . . .		,,
Lampe, Mrs. W. E.		,,
Miller, Rev. H.K., 1892		Yamagata
Miller, Mrs. H.K.		,,
Moore, Rev. J.P., D.D., 1883,*. . .		Tokyo
Moore, Mrs. J.P.		,,
Noss, Rev. C., 1895,. , .	in U.S.	Sendai
Noss, Mrs. C., ...	,, ,. .	,,
Schneder, Rev. D.B., D.D., 1887 . .		,,
Schneder, Mrs. D.B.		,,
Snyder, Rev. S.S., 1894 . .	in U.S.	,,
Snyder, Mrs. S.S. . . .	,, ,, .	,,
Stick, Rev. J.M., 1902		,,
Stick, Mrs. J.M.		,,
Pifer, Miss Catherine, 1901. . . .		Sendai
Powell, Miss Lucy M., 1900 . . .		,,
Weidner, Miss Sadie Lea, 1900 . . .		,,
Zurfluh, Miss Lena, 1894		,,

MISSION OF THE CUMBERLAND PRESBYTERIAN CHURCH

Hail, Rev. A.D., D.D., 1878* . . .		Osaka
Hail, Mrs. A.D.,*		,,
Hail. Rev. J.B., D.D., 1877 .	in U.S.	Wakayama

Hail, Mrs. J.B.	in U.S.	Wakayama
Hail, Rev. J.E., 1900*		Tsu
Lathom, Rev. H.L., 1902*		,,
Lathom, Mrs. H.L.*		,,
Hereford, Rev. W.F., 1902*		Wakayama
Hereford, Mrs. W.F.*		,,
Van Horn, Rev. G.W., 1888		Osaka
Van Horn, Mrs. G.W.		,,
Worley, Rev. J.C., 1899*		Yamada
Worley, Mrs. J.C.*		,,
Alexander, Miss S., 1894	in U.S.	Osaka
Gardner, Miss Ella, 1893	,, ,,	Tanabe
Leavitt, Miss Julia, 1881*		,,
Lyons, Mrs. N.A., 1894	in U.S.	Osaka
Morgan, Miss Agnes E., 1889		,,
Ranson, Miss Mary E., 1901		,,
Hail, Miss A.N., 1902* (Associate Member).		,,

WOMANS UNION MISSIONARY SOCIETY

Crosby, Miss Julia N., 1871	Yokohama
Hand, Miss Julia E., 1900.	,,
Loomis, Miss Clara D., 1901	,,
Pratt, Miss S.A., 1893	,,
Strain, Miss Helen Knox, 1900	,,
Tracey, Miss Mary E., 1903	,,

www.ingramcontent.com/pod-product-compliance
Lightning Source LLC
Chambersburg PA
CBHW031407160426
43196CB00007B/925